Principles of
R&D
Management

PRINCIPLES OF
R&D
MANAGEMENT

Philip H. Francis

amacom A Division of American Management Associations

Library of Congress Cataloging in Publication Data
Francis, Philip H
  Principles of R&D management.

  Bibliography: p.
  Includes index.
  1. Research—Management. I. Title.
Q180.55.M3F7   658′.91′00143   77-24179
ISBN 0-8144-5451-8

First Printing

In dedication to . . .

My lovely wife, Diana, and to our four extraordinary children—Scott, Edward, Mary, and Kenneth, all of whom made many sacrifices so I could adjust my priorities.

PREFACE

Just as necessity is the mother of invention, this book was born of a need for a single reference source from which to teach a graduate course on research and development (R&D) management. Although some books touch on various aspects of this rather broad area, I found none that provided the scope and the proper blend of management principles together with the pragmatic approach which I considered necessary to meet the needs of that course. Moreover, I believe there is a need for a management primer in the field of R&D which could easily and usefully be read by professionals working at the interface between technology and business. Scientists and engineers today who are catapulted from the familiar context of their technical fields to the "interface" find, as I did some years ago, that there is a good deal to learn about management and its applications in their technological environment. While I stand firmly convinced that management must be practiced in order to be learned, the beginner who is equipped with a good guidebook can save a lot of time and develop some helpful skills along the way. I trust that the judgment of time will prove this work to be an adequate guidebook.

The five chapters which comprise this book were written to be independent units, so that they can be read in part or in full in any chosen order. The possible exception is Chapter 1, which provides an important backdrop for the remaining chapters by describing the kinds of institutions engaged in modern R&D, the major sources and uses of R&D funding, and the broad responsibilities of R&D managers. The rest of the book addresses the organizational, behavioral, entrepreneurial, and legal aspects of R&D, which are the most basic and important issues to which management must be attuned. In each chapter, I have attempted to draw together some of the fundamental principles from management theory and integrate them with the practical focus used in the management process as applied to technology. Thus, the treatment attempts to strike a balance between a discourse on abstract theory and a handbook on problem solving, neither of which is appropriate in itself.

In keeping with this theme, I have avoided going into several technical aspects of R&D management where the emphasis is on tools—for example, the budget process, capital investment, and payoff measurement. Techniques which have been applied to these and other subjects are treated in some of the references described in the annotated bibliography and elsewhere in the book. Also, the presentation is somewhat specialized in that it is essentially tailored to U.S. technology. In the near future the growing practice of R&D across national boundaries will undoubtedly require additional treatment in updated publications.

In undertaking this book, I have been influenced by many writers and colleagues, too many to mention, and I hope the result does credit to them. There are, however, several associates who deserve particular recognition. Dr. James E. Ashton, Director of Manufacturing Management Support at the Ft. Worth Division of General Dynamics Corp., read the entire manuscript and made many important suggestions. A young man of outstanding scholarship and accomplishment in both engineering and management, and a good personal friend as well, his influence pervades much of this book. Appreciation is also extended to those who graciously consented to read and criticize various portions of the manuscript. Professor David L. Wilemon of the Syracuse University School of Management made many helpful comments on organizational structure and on project and matrix management in Chapter 2. Gus N. Van Steenberg, Patent Attorney at Southwest Research Institute, provided a careful review and valuable expansion of portions of Chapter 5. Richard S. Woodbury, Corporate Counsel of Southwest Research Institute, also provided very useful advice on legal matters addressed in Chapter 5.

Others to whom I am indebted include Herbert I. Hoffman and Robert E. Chatten of Southwest Research Institute, and H. Dana Moran of Battelle Memorial Institute. Dr. Harvey Thomas, consulting industrial psychologist, inspired the treatment of the hiring process in Chapter 3 and has encouraged me in my endeavor from the beginning. Dr. Ralph G. H. Siu, former Deputy Director of the Research and Engineering Directorate, Army Materiel Command, graciously consented to allow me to use several of his proverbs (which, in his words, "are, after all, not mine but belong to the ages") to introduce the chapters. Finally, I am especially indebted to my several hundred students in the Systems Management Program at St. Mary's University who, over a four-year period, served as a collective sounding board and provided portions of the research data needed to bring this effort to fruition. Despite these invaluable sources of counsel, I accept full responsibility for any deficiency of logic, balance, or fact.

One final word. I trust none of my readers will be offended by my consistent and exclusive use of the masculine pronoun and possessive adjective. I have done this neither to incite nor to foster chauvinism, but merely to simplify style.

Philip H. Francis

CONTENTS

THE R&D 1
MANAGEMENT
ENVIRONMENT

The good executive not only brings home the bacon, but also the applesauce.

Few would dispute the claim that the United States and the other advanced nations of the world have achieved their economic and political strength largely through technology. The quickening pace with which science and technology influence our lives, solve and create social problems, and provide mankind with the human comforts it desires is difficult to grasp. We all are inexorably caught up in technology's wake as society struggles to adapt to a continuously changing world dominated by technology. Public consciousness of the power of what Alvin Toffler has called the modern "superindustrial society" is at an all-time high. People fear it, criticize it, attempt to escape from it, and often expect too much of technology in providing pleasant solutions to unpleasant problems. In the final analysis, however, the fruits of technology are indeed plentiful. Through better understanding and management of advanced technology, society can inherit a legacy of promise for all people.

THE HIGH-TECHNOLOGY ARENA

Modern technology is a process which is largely conducted by R&D teams operating within a dynamic, innovative environment. Technology is created by diverse missions and needs. The requirements for teams of highly skilled scientists, engineers, and technicians has led to an unprecedented management environment where the employee often has more highly developed

1

technical skills in his area of specialty than his supervisor has. This climate has focused attention on the professional technologist as a manager of highly talented employees, and constitutes a management responsibility that is unusually challenging.

The rapid growth of technology in the western world has been fostered by the joint contributions of government and industry. The federal government, as the embodiment of the people it serves, has as its basic technological mission to maintain and enhance the health, security, and well-being of its citizens. Traditionally, in the United States, this mission has been most visibly pursued in the development of advanced military systems. To an increasing extent, however, the government is focusing its technological resources on such areas as environmental preservation, energy recovery, public health, and the transfer of military and space technology to other public purposes. In addition to its great influence in nurturing applied R&D, the government also supports a broad program in basic research to ensure long-term technological strength through the potential of discovery.

The corporate and private economic sectors have played an important complementary role in technological development. Here, of course, the objectives are different: survival of the organization itself (profit motive) is paramount, followed by obligations to employees' well-being and society at large. Because the missions of commercial organizations vis-à vis those of the federal government differ, so then do their influences in technological development. Industrial R&D is necessarily short-range. Basic research is too risky in terms of payoff and is too long-range to warrant substantial investment by private industry. Rather, industrial R&D is geared toward supporting product development in the near term, to strengthen the organization's position in the marketplace.

Several years ago the Brookings Institution published a study which showed that of the 100 leading U.S. companies in 1909, only 36 were still in business 40 years later. Those 36 survivors were characterized as having aggressive R&D programs closely coupled with the continual introduction of new customer-satisfying products. Those organizations which expired or came to be absorbed by stronger companies generally lacked effective R&D support. Contemporary industrialism is even more tightly linked to applied research for the technology base on which new products and markets can be exploited. Thus, it is more important than ever that R&D management in the commercial sector understand technology's role in today's dynamic, competitive marketing environment.

There are many different forms of organizations which perform R&D today.* Nearly all fall into one of the categories listed below:

Government Laboratories. The federal R&D complex is vast indeed. It includes several interservice agencies of the Department of Defense, such as the Advanced Research Projects Agency (ARPA), although these are primarily for R&D planning, administration, and contracting. Each of the armed services has its own R&D complex. The Navy Department has several centers, such as the Naval Ship R&D Center and the Naval Surface Weapons Center, responsible for applied mission-oriented efforts. In addition, there are the laboratories—for example, the Naval Research Laboratory and the Naval Civil Engineering Laboratory—where work of a more fundamental nature is conducted. The Army also maintains its own mission-oriented commands, such as the U.S. Army Missile Command, Medical R&D Command, Armament Command, and Natick R&D Command, as well as discipline-oriented laboratories including the Harry Diamond Laboratories and the Air Mobility R&D Laboratory. The Air Force conducts its own R&D program within major commands (such as the Air Force Systems Command) and laboratories (such as the Air Force Weapons Laboratory).

Federal "in-house" R&D is not limited, of course, to the Armed Services departments. The National Aeronautics and

---

* The history of modern technological growth is fascinating, and many books have been written on the current scope and structure of the "military-industrial complex." One of the best and most recent is that of the late Dr. Harold Vagtborg.[1]

Space Administration (NASA) conducts a vigorous space-related program divided among its Research Centers (Ames, Lewis, and Langley), its Flight Centers and other assembly and test facilities, and the Jet Propulsion Laboratory, operated by the California Institute of Technology under contract to NASA. Other federal laboratories which conduct important research programs on a large scale include the Sandia Laboratories, the Los Alamos Scientific Laboratory, the National Bureau of Standards, and the Oak Ridge National Laboratory. All these, and many more not mentioned here, are government-owned facilities whose budgets and objectives are set by the federal government. Much of the work is conducted in house and ranges in scope from fundamental research to applied and developmental technology.

Federal Contract Research Centers. Also known as "captive organizations," the FCRCs are permanent facilities, established for the purpose of conducting studies, advising and consulting, and aiding in policy making on behalf of their sponsoring agencies. There are at present some 75 FCRCs, of which RAND, the Aerospace Corporation, MITRE, and the recently formed Solar Energy Research Institute (SERI) are among the best-known examples. These organizations are set up as not-for-profit institutions and may perform services for many other agencies. The determinant for being classified as an FCRC is that the organization have a principal (though not necessarily exclusive) and continuing obligation to one sponsoring federal agency.

Not-for-Profit Institutions. These organizations, which may be publicly or privately owned, occupy a position midway between academic research and R&D as performed in a profit-making organization. There are currently more than 5,000 such institutions throughout the United States, including the larger ones such as Battelle Memorial Institute, Stanford Research Institute, Southwest Research Institute, Illinois Institute of Technology Research Institute, and Hudson Institute. Research is conducted for government and commercial clients under contract or grant, and all fees ("profits") that may be derived from project work are plowed back into the institution for additional capital equipment and facilities. There are no stockholders to share in the distribution of profits.

These organizations, which are distinguished from the FCRCs in that they do not depend on a single federal agency for primary and continuing support, are exempted from federal income taxes on all work performed "in the public interest." That is, all work other than proprietary R&D conducted for commercial organizations where the results are not made generally available to the public is tax exempt. Inasmuch as not-for-profit R&D institutions do not have the same profit demands placed on them as profit-making organizations do, they are often in a better position to engage in basic or developmental research where profits are marginal. Nevertheless, they are essentially business organizations and must produce quality R&D services under strict management control in order to maintain and expand their technical facilities.

Independent Nonprofit Organizations. There are a handful of truly independent nonprofit research organizations which are funded by private supporters and donations. These organizations, such as the Brookings Institution and the Center for the Study of Democratic Institutions, serve an important role in helping shape public opinion, particularly in broad areas of national and international policy.

Corporate R&D Laboratories. Nearly all corporations which manufacture products of high technology, especially those associated with the defense, aerospace, transportation, and energy-related industries, have their own research laboratories. These are maintained for purposes of supporting manufacturing and marketing operations, and are funded largely from corporate profits. Budgets are allocated and activities are selected for those projects which are judged to be most beneficial to the technological requirements of the organization.

Whereas scientists and engineers working in such laboratories are occasionally permitted to seek outside contract support for their research interests, the major thrusts of the efforts are company related. As a result, research activities tend to be along more applied, product-oriented lines. The organizational structure of such laboratories varies widely according to the size and degree of long-range commitment the parent company gives to R&D. Many small and medium-size companies have a single department focused on one development project. Large corporations often set up an entire R&D organization separate from the parent company; the organization may be accountable to a single budget allocated by the parent company, or it may derive part of its operating funds from government R&D contracts.

Educational Institutions. Public and private universities and academic institutions perform a substantial portion of the nation's fundamental R&D in order to give faculty and students continuing exposure to scientific and engineering research. Many public universities operate research laboratories or experiment stations where contract research is carried out largely by faculty and graduate students on a part-time basis. Whereas state institutions are tied to their respective legislatures for operating funds, private universities must aggressively seek federal research contract support to help defray expenses as well as to provide intellectual stimulus. Differences exist among all academic institutions as to how faculty salaries are apportioned between institutional and contract funds. Academic institutions tend to have more modest capital equipment investments than government and commercial organizations but can perform certain kinds of fundamental R&D of high quality and (generally) at less cost.

Private Profit-Making Institutions. Private organizations which exist for the purpose of making a profit on contract R&D have an advantage over academic institutions in that such organizations devote their entire resources to R&D. Also, they can attract outstanding researchers who do not wish to divide their time between teaching and research. Since their costs tend to be high, the private profit-making R&D institutions must be keen, business-oriented opportunists in order to prosper.

There are approximately 300 such organizations operating today, most of which are engaged principally in paper studies and consultancy. Arthur D. Little, Inc., Systems Development Corporation, Booz, Allen & Hamilton Inc., Calspan (formerly Cornell Aeronautical Laboratory), and the Diebold Group are some of the more widely known profit-making research institutions. In addition to those institutions engaged solely in R&D, many independent laboratories throughout the United States are engaged primarily in testing. These laboratories concentrate on certifying materials and equipment and on routine testing and analysis for the federal government and for industry.

These are the principal players in the contemporary technology arena. Each has an important interacting role to play in contributing to the development of new technology. In the complex, continually changing R&D structure in the United States, an effective R&D management must keep in close touch with all aspects of the total high-technology endeavor: clients, competitors, and human and capital resources. This challenge places great responsibility on R&D managers at all levels, not only for planning and operations, but also for carefully observing changing patterns and trends within the R&D establishment.

SCOPE OF R&D IN THE UNITED STATES

Figure 1-1 broadly summarizes the current national effort in research and development.[2] The total funding for all R&D efforts in the United States approached $35 billion in 1975, or about 2.3 percent of the gross national product (GNP). There are several ways of evaluating this level of commitment to R&D. In terms of current dollars, the total R&D annual expenditure has been increasing steadily since the early 1950s, although when referenced to fixed dollars (i.e., accounting for inflation), the R&D investment has been declining in recent years. (See Figure 1-2.) This decreasing trend holds true also for the proportion of the GNP devoted to R&D; in 1964, 3 percent of it went to R&D, but this fell to 2.3 percent in 1975, and is estimated to remain at that level through 1977. This trend is seen as due primarily to reduced growth of federal R&D expenditures in the defense and space areas. Increases in R&D funds from all other sources, however, combined to keep pace with the overall growth in the GNP.

Of the 53 percent of all R&D funds which were allocated by the federal government in 1975, more than half were actually spent by industry, mostly in national defense and space exploration. That is, government-supported R&D in the private sector was at an annual level of about $9 to $10 billion, or some 0.6 percent of the GNP. Adding this federal support to industry's own annual investment in R&D shows that about 70 percent of

Figure 1-1. The national R&D effort.

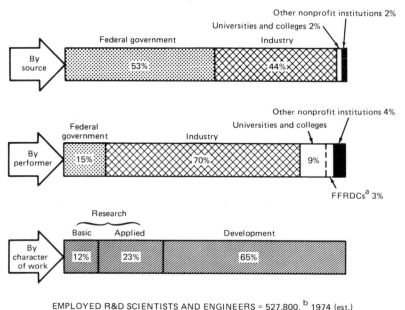

EXPENDITURES FOR R&D = $34.3 BILLION, 1975 (est.)

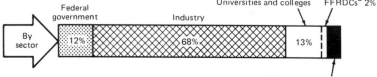

[a]Federally funded research and development centers administered by universities and colleges.

[b]Full-time equivalents.

SOURCE: National Science Foundation Report NSF 75-307, "National Patterns of R&D Resources: Funds and Manpower in the United States, 1953–1975."

all funds devoted to R&D in 1975 were actually spent by private industry. As indicated by Figure 1-1, the proportions of the total national R&D budget actually spent (rather than merely contributed) by the federal government, by colleges and universities, and by other institutions were quite small by comparison. Thus R&D performance, although dominated by the corporate industrial sector, is strongly influenced by the commitment of federal R&D funds.

In examining the principal technical components of the total R&D activity in the United States, it is useful to have some breakdown of the areas in which funds are allocated. Government expenditures for R&D are classified by the Organization for Economic Cooperation and Development (OECD) into a collection of categories suitable for this purpose[3]:

National Defense—encompassing all R&D directly related to military purposes, including space and nuclear energy activities of a military character.

Space—including all civilian space R&D such as manned space flight programs and scientific investigations in space.

Figure 1-2. National R&D funding trends, 1953–1975.

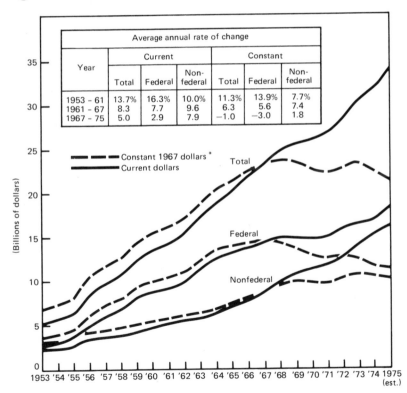

* The GNP implicit price deflator has been used to convert from current to constant dollars.

SOURCE: National Science Foundation Report NSF 75-307, "National Patterns of R&D Resources: Funds and Manpower in the United States, 1953–1975."

Health—encompassing R&D in all the medical sciences and in health management.

Economic Development—which covers R&D in a wide range of fields including agriculture, forestry, and fisheries; mining and manufacturing; and transportation, communications, construction, and utilities.

Community Services—which includes R&D for such purposes as pollution control, education, social services, disaster prevention, planning, and statistics.

Nuclear Energy—consisting of all civilian R&D primarily concerned with nuclear sciences and technology.

Advancement of Science—consisting of funds for fundamental research in government and private laboratories, and for research and science instruction in universities.

The relative commitment of funds to these categories for the fiscal year 1971–1972 is illustrated in Figure 1-3. The percentages shown are typical of the distribution of funding for other recent years.

Whereas the federal government allocates substantial funds to meet needs in the basic and applied research areas, private industry commits the bulk of its R&D funds to product development. Most industrial R&D is concentrated in a few manufacturing industries, especially in communications equipment, aerospace, motor vehicles and other transportation systems, chemicals, and machinery.[4] Within these industries, most of the R&D strength is in the hands of a relatively small number of large industries that dominate the markets (i.e., an oligarchic system). Industrial R&D is viewed within each organization as one kind of investment which must compete for funds and resources with alternative investment opportunities. Thus, the majority of the industrial R&D budget goes toward supporting product development, with less than 5 percent allocated to basic research.

The support of our contemporary technological society, then, relies heavily on the federal government for long-range R&D activities, and on the industrial sector for short-range development capabilities. As indicated previously, industry, not the federal government, is now the prime source of funds for industrial R&D. This trend has been steady over the past two decades and results in more stable budgets for development work. Industrial commitments to basic research, on the other hand, have remained

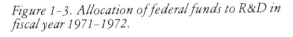

Figure 1-3. Allocation of federal funds to R&D in fiscal year 1971-1972.

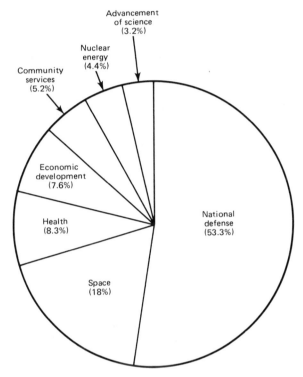

SOURCE: "Science Indicators—1974," Report of the National Science Board of the National Science Foundation, 1975.

small and relatively unchanged: about 2 percent of total national R&D expenditures. The majority of all basic research (55 percent) is conducted by universities and is supported largely by the federal government. The proportion of all funds allocated to different types of R&D activities—basic research, applied research, and development—has remained nearly constant since the mid-1960s. In recent years, however, R&D has been directed increasingly to nondefense and nonspace purposes, such as the development of new energy resources, conservation, and environmental protection.

Table 1-1. Distribution of scientists and engineers employed in R&D by sector, 1974.

SECTOR	PERCENT
Industry	68
Federal government	13
Universities and colleges	12
Other nonprofit institutions	5
FFRDCs*	2
Total	100

* University-associated federally funded research and development centers.
SOURCE: National Science Foundation Report NSF 75-307, "National Patterns of R&D Resources: Funds and Manpower in the United States, 1953–1975."

Having described the complexion of national R&D funding, it is appropriate to indicate the size of the scientific labor force which transforms those budgets into technology. In 1974 about 528,000 scientists and engineers, or 25 per 10,000 population,* were engaged in R&D activities on a full-time equivalent basis in all sectors of the economy (excluding state and local governments). This number represents approximately one-third of the estimated total employment of 1.7 million scientists and engineers. These figures have held relatively constant in recent years, with engineers accounting for nearly two-thirds of the total.[2,3] The distribution of this R&D labor force is summarized in Table 1-1, and shows that the large majority of those working in R&D are employed in the industrial sector.

The statistics cited above serve to outline the dimensions of research and development activities in the United States, but do not indicate the output therefrom. The benefits of R&D are difficult to measure in specific terms since they issue from so many different sources and embrace the whole spectrum from basic research through product/systems development.

* This is the highest proportion among all technologically developed nations except for the USSR, where the figure is estimated to be about 37 per 10,000 population.[3]

Some indication can be achieved, however, by contrasting technological invention with the products of innovation. Technological invention is the process of discovering new physical principles on which development can later be built. Inventions represent real or potential advances in technology. Typically, the time lag between first conception (invention) and innovation (development) averages about six years, but varies widely depending on potential market impact and technological sophistication. One crude measure of invention is the number of patents granted annually by the United States and foreign governments to U.S. scientists and engineers. This measure can be indicative of the progress of only those inventions which consist of a synthesis of existing technological processes, and therefore may more correctly be termed innovation.

The number of patents granted to U.S. scientists and engineers has been rising dramatically in recent decades. Of course, only a small fraction of such patents ultimately reach the marketplace. The number of patents granted falls short of indicating the true strength of inventiveness, however, since the United States and other advanced technological nations grant patents to foreign nationals. It is therefore useful to consider the *patent balance,* that is, the difference between the number of foreign patents granted to U.S. nationals and the number of U.S. patents granted to foreign nationals.

Statistics of this sort compiled by the National Science Foundation[3] show that the United States has enjoyed a favorable but declining patent balance since the mid-1960s. In 1973, for example, approximately 41,000 foreign patents were granted to U.S. scientists and engineers, whereas only 15,000 U.S. patents were awarded to foreign nationals, leading to a patent balance of 26,000. Further, the patent balance fell by about 30 percent during the period 1966–1973, suggesting that the number of patentable ideas of international merit has been growing in other countries at a greater rate than in the United States.

Technological innovation is somewhat more difficult to measure. Innovation is the process whereby existing technologies and principles are fused together in new ways to produce new and improved products, systems, and processes. Acquiring the technology underlying innovation is a complex process involving

basic and applied research, technology transfer from other product lines, and corporate licensing, mergers, and acquisitions.
Again, the National Science Foundation has developed certain
yardsticks which attempt to measure innovation productivity.[3]

Available data indicate that the United States has consistently
led other developed nations of the world in the relative number
of major technological innovations produced. This is especially
true of the most R&D-intensive industries, such as electronics,
electrical equipment and communications, chemical and allied
products, machinery, and professional and scientific instruments.
Over the years large companies have produced more technological innovations than smaller companies have, although the opposite is true for innovations per unit sales. Small firms play a major
role in the innovative process, and generally achieve growth
through continuing innovative developments.

As with invention, technological innovation crosses national
boundaries. A substantial amount of technological know-how is
bought and sold internationally, especially between multinational companies and their foreign affiliates, but also among independent organizations. The United States receives substantially more than it pays out for patents, manufacturing rights,
licenses, and so on, and this *technological balance* is growing
larger with time. In 1974 the ratio of receipts to payout was approximately 5:1, the largest in recent history. Nevertheless, the
volume of know-how imported by U.S. organizations is substantial and is expanding in several areas, notably in plastics, machine tools, and mining processes.

It has been reliably estimated that more than half of the annual
increase in national productivity is due to scientific, engineering,
and industrial advances and to improved methods of managing
technology. In terms of the world balance of trade (exports minus
imports), the United States has seen a fourfold increase in R&D-
intensive products since 1960, to $25 billion in 1974. Most of this
increase has come from electrical and nonelectrical machinery,
aircraft, chemicals, and instruments. In contrast, the United
States has seen a large and increasing trade deficit in non-R&D-
intensive products, such as motor vehicles, textiles, and metals.

Science and technology today have become truly international
efforts, as suggested by the preceding discussion. Research—both

basic and applied—is a continuing process which builds on previous results obtained and reported worldwide. This internationalism of communications channels serves to reduce wasteful redundancy in R&D efforts and to achieve efficiency through collaborative efforts. Cooperative efforts are fostered both formally and informally by publications, international meetings, and the personal communications they precipitate. As a result, science and technology—today more than ever before—transcend political boundaries and help bring about increased understanding among the different peoples of the world.

ROLE OF THE R&D MANAGER

In a book whose purpose is to deal with some of the key aspects of professional management, it is appropriate to provide background on the scope of the management process. What exactly is management? Certainly the term means various things to various people. To some, the designation manager suggests one who acts as a caretaker of assets (people, money, and things) and who makes decisions regarding their disposition. Indeed, these are proper responsibilities of all managers. However, in today's dynamic and aggressive technological environment much more is expected of the R&D manager than simply to act as an organization caretaker; the term *administrator* more appropriately characterizes that function. Among the many facets of management which might serve to strike a contrast between the passive act of administration and the active process of management, several will be touched on here.

Management is today a very broad and diverse field, and as such defies a succinct and adequate definition. It has often been described as the job of "getting things done through people." This interpretation emphasizes the manager as a goal setter, as having authority over people, and as a mobilizer of people for the purpose of goal attainment. It therefore suggests that management is a *process*, that is, a sequence of coordinated events.

In contrast to that interpretation of a manager's function, Reddin has provided a formal definition in terms of organizational status:[5] "A manager is a person occupying a position in a formal organization who is responsible for the work of at least one other person and who has authority over that person." While this may serve as an acceptable definition, it is more useful to consider the manager as a person whose function is to fulfill four basic responsibilities:

Planning—Setting appropriate objectives, then selecting courses of action which are most likely to result in the effective fulfillment of those objectives.

Organizing—Implementing the planning function by establishing structure, procedures, and resource requirements.

Directing—Coordinating employees' activities and, through effective leadership, ensuring proper execution of group assignments.

Controlling—Keeping the operation on its intended course by providing checks on key activities, comparing these results against suitable standards, and directing changes where necessary.

These responsibilities are quite broad and therefore require that the manager be imaginative, resourceful, and flexible in his approach to them. He must also demonstrate leadership in every aspect of his job in order that his subordinates can willingly give the organization their best efforts.

Because of their close interrelationship, these four responsibilities—planning, organizing, directing, and controlling—characterize management as a process. The components of the process must all be integrated and carried out smoothly in order to mobilize assets for the accomplishment of goals. In contrast to these varied responsibilities of the manager, the administrator focuses only on directing, and is less responsible for planning, organizing, and controlling, as these fall largely outside his area of cognizance.*

The field of management is currently a blend of art and science, and certainly offers the manager less in the way of specific tools than physics offers the physicist. It has been only recently that quantitative models have found their way into practice, thereby giving management at least the appearance of a science. In point of fact, however, some of the original thinkers in the field long ago attempted to quantify the management process. Frederick Taylor, who is frequently called the "father of scientific management," elucidated his then unorthodox ideas concerning ra-

* Mayhall provides an excellent outline of the administrative aspects of R&D management.[6]

tional and efficient management in his books *Shop Management* (1906) and *The Principles of Scientific Management* (1911). Frank and Lillian Gilbreth shortly thereafter developed the science of time and motion analysis and the psychology of management.

By the early 1920s the term "scientific management" had become an established international "buzz word," widely employed to describe a variety of organizational processes ranging from work flow on the shop floor to Lenin's overthrow of czarist Russia. However, those early efforts to create a management science were applied narrowly to labor masses in industrialized circumstances and have not established a sufficiently comprehensive basis for the practice of management in today's high-technology environment. Thus the effective practice of management—particularly R&D management—relies heavily on the manager's skillful art of working with and leading people.

In the ensuing decades management has evolved into a discipline to be practiced at all levels of the organization, not only by the chief executive. This evolution has come about largely because of the emergence and dominance of the corporate form of organization and the consequent separation of control from ownership. This trend has created a need for professional managers whose financial interest is far less than controlling, and whose effectiveness is measured not by how many dollars they bring in today but by their accomplishments over the long term.

The technical disciplines of science and engineering, which used to be quite distinct, have moved much closer together since World War II. Team R&D has appeared, and consequently the individual has been subordinated to the requirements of the project group. The broad field of R&D as practiced today has produced a manager who not only is trained and experienced in technology but is effective in carrying out the responsibilities of the management process as well. He is a synergistic person who must use his combined technical and managerial capabilities both to lead people and to help steer his organization safely through the turbulent tides of technology.

The R&D manager must have the ability to define the relationship of his group's activities to overall organization goals. This is particularly true at higher levels of management, where the emphasis is on developing broad policy, evaluating overall performance, and making nonroutine decisions. He must be sensitive to the legitimate contribution of his R&D efforts to the organization as viewed by his own supervisor, the chief executive, the stockholders or federal administrators, and the citizens and taxpayers to whom he is ultimately accountable.

To fill his role adequately in the dynamic climate of modern technology, the R&D manager must also be an opportunist. This means he must have the capacity to seize and exploit opportunities as they arise. Moreover, since R&D efforts are not always amenable to deliberate and consistent planning, the effective manager must have the awareness needed to help shape events to his own advantage. This theme has been emphasized by Peter Drucker,[7] who stresses that results can be attained only by identifying and exploiting opportunities; the resources of any organization should therefore be allocated to opportunities rather than to problems. The question should be *what to pursue*, rather than *how to proceed*. This approach requires that the manager continually reassess the results of his activities in relation to potential opportunities on the horizon.

Having described the general demands placed on the R&D manager, it is appropriate to determine what characteristics the organization should exhibit to be creative, vital, and ongoing. There is a wide diversity of R&D organizations, of course, so it is difficult to be specific. Nevertheless, it is possible to sketch a profile of a productive R&D organization that is meaningful to the manager. The following list is drawn from the comprehensive study made by Ranftl[8] in 1973–1974. It characterizes the productive R&D organization as possessing five basic attributes:

Effectively Staffed and People-Oriented. Such an organization has outstanding key people, challenges its employees and is sensitive to their needs, and recognizes their accomplishments.

Has High Standards. The organization operates with high standards of ethics and integrity, and fulfills schedule, cost, and performance requirements faithfully.

Operates in a Sound and Competitive Manner. The organization is committed to adherence to established goals, operates profitably, and maintains a sound business backlog with a proper balance of operations.

Provides a Creative and Productive Atmosphere. The organization
encourages innovation, is free of stifling controls, and furnishes
adequate and up-to-date facilities and equipment.

Manifests Enthusiasm with a "Can Do" Attitude. The productive
organization's employees act in harmony as a loyal team, anxious to
tackle new opportunities with confidence and commitment.

These characteristics serve as a handy checklist for evaluating a
high-technology organization for productivity. Significant deviations from one or more of these standards usually signal impend-
ing problems that must be recognized and dealt with. Thus, as a
key figure in creating the style and effectiveness of the organization, the R&D manager must constantly be aware of his relationship with the organization.

The discussion above has indicated some of the qualities expected of the effective R&D manager. The tremendous impact
modern technology has made on all segments of modern society
has created a need for a new legion of leaders. Much is required of
these leaders. They must, first of all, be men and women of
superior technical accomplishments. Moreover, to fulfill their
role in the management process, they must be effective as
businessmen, administrators, entrepreneurs, and social psychologists. And finally, they must be tough-minded—able to make
hard decisions when events so require.

Despite the pace of technological accomplishment, society has
yet to develop effective training programs for this new breed of
leaders. This training gap is perhaps the most serious obstacle to
be overcome in bringing technology to its full potential. In the
past, managers of R&D have been chosen more on the basis of
seniority and technical excellence than on their promise as managers. This practice has been shortsighted and has produced
many technical managers who have been ill equipped to be man-
ager-leaders and have felt frustrated working outside the main-
stream of technical practice.

At present there is still no satisfactory substitute for experience,
although technical societies are increasingly developing new
and effective programs, seminars, and short courses for the purpose of grounding R&D managers in the principles of management. Graduate schools of business and administration have so

far met with only modest success in providing useful training for managers of technology. Indeed, studies have shown an alarming lack of correlation between academic achievement in M.B.A. and related programs and later success in managerial effectiveness. This is a harsh indictment that can be overcome only if a better knowledge of managerial requirements is coupled with innovative educational programs designed to produce the skills and awareness needed.

REFERENCES

1. Harold Vagtborg, *Research and American Industrial Development: A Bicentennial Look at the Contributions of Applied R&D*. New York: Pergamon Press, 1976.
2. "National Patterns of R&D Resources: Funds and Manpower in the United States, 1953–1975," National Science Foundation Report NSF 75-307.
3. "Science Indicators—1974," Report of the National Science Board of the National Science Foundation, 1975.
4. "Where Private Industry Puts Its Research Money," *Business Week*, June 28, 1976.
5. W. J. Reddin, *Managerial Effectiveness*. New York: McGraw-Hill Book Co., Inc., 1970.
6. William Mayhall, *Corporate R&D Administration*, AMA Research Study 102, American Management Associations, 1970.
7. Peter F. Drucker, *Managing for Results*. New York: Harper & Row, 1964.
8. Robert M. Ranftl, "R&D Productivity—A Key Issue," *Astronautics & Aeronautics*, June 1976, pp. 50–56.

ELEMENTS OF ORGANIZATION THEORY

2

It is not the final blow of the ax that fells the tree.

The need to organize collective behavior within human social and economic structures is part of the spirit of man. Evidence exists to suggest that the ancient Egyptians, in undertaking such mammoth construction projects as the Great Pyramid of Giza, had developed organizational systems not too unlike many of today's. As civilization itself continued to unfold, many new aspects of human endeavor requiring organization emerged, such as agriculture and farming, crafts and construction, and manufacturing. Along with these developments, man's legal, religious, and other institutions grew in complexity, and all these processes posed unique organizational problems. It is difficult to conceive of social and economic systems even within a utopian society which could function effectively without some form of organizational structure.

FORMAL ORGANIZATION THEORY

Inherent to any group endeavor is the concept of organization. An organization serves to bind the various individuals in the endeavor and integrate their separate activities along a single direction to achieve common goals. Organization accomplishes this first by mobilizing diverse resources within the structure. More than that, however, it is a mechanism for countering those competitive forces which would undermine human collaboration. It is designed to minimize or resolve conflicts and neutralize the effect of individual behavior which deviates from group standards;

21

and it attempts to do this, moreover, without stifling individual creativity. Finally, organization introduces stability into intragroup relationships by reducing uncertainty regarding the nature of group structure and the individual roles within it.

The importance of effective organization within modern industrial and government agencies need not be emphasized. Within recent years great strides have been made in creating new organizational forms especially suited to particular purposes. Some of those which have been applied to high-technology organizations are described in later sections of this chapter. However, these hybrid forms of organization must usually function within what has come to be known as the "host" or formal organizational structure, and this particular framework is the subject of the present section.

Traditional organization theory concerns the structure and interaction of organizational components and the people staffing them. Considerations of human personalities and their interactions—the purview of the behavioral sciences—are treated separately, in Chapter 3. However, before beginning the treatment of traditional organization theory, it is useful to have a clear understanding of some terms commonly used to discuss the exercise of human behavior within an organizational structure.

The Authority System

In particular, the terms *power, authority,* and *influence* are often used to describe the interactive processes among individuals and groups of individuals within organizations. These and related terms spring from the basic concept of an *authority system,* which refers to the manner in which decisions are made and promulgated within an organization or segment of society.

Such a system has several features.[1] To begin with, it functions in a hierarchical structure in which a few make decisions for the relatively many. These decisions fall into two general categories. One concerns standing decisions, that is, policies and procedures intended to be followed uniformly over a long period of time. The other deals with ad hoc decisions, which are handed down by executives and are meant to interpret standing decisions or to fashion rules not already covered by standing decisions. All decisions, whether standing or ad hoc, are communicated in an authority system from the executives (the few) to their subordinates (the many). The subordinates, in turn, are motivated by various means to carry out the decisions handed them by management.

Power, authority, and influence are exercised continuously at all hierarchical levels within organizations. In describing these three terms it is perhaps best to consider them in reverse order. *Influence* is used to describe the ability to control others by suggestion or example rather than by direct command. It exists not by virtue of the formal supervisor-employee relationship, but by the unconscious choice of one person to emulate a behavioral pattern suggested or manifested by another. *Authority* refers to the formal right to issue orders or directives by virtue of one's position in the organizational structure; it is thus granted to (or withdrawn from) a person strictly within the organizational environment, and becomes effective only if it is accepted. Closely related to authority is the concept of responsibility or accountability, which indicates the perceived commitment or obligation to fulfill assigned duties. Responsibility is nourished by authority, and cannot exist effectively without the right to act or control. *Power*, on the other hand, implies the ability (not necessarily the right) to control behavior. Power may exist by virtue of expertise, interest, charisma, or such strategic factors as coalitions or location.

Power, authority, and influence are all latent forces in that no control is effected unless they are activated. They are independent, but highly interactive. Effective management requires a balanced blend of all three forces, for when any one looms dominant over the others the result usually is administrative disorder.

Basic Management Principles

Good management practice reflects the recognition over time that a common set of basic principles is present in most effectively run organizations. Some have held that these principles should be considered as axioms—basic and generally accepted requirements that, taken together, form the basis for a consistent and logical structure known as "good management." This view, however, probably ascribes more scientific content to the field of management than it actually contains at the present time. The eight principles described below should therefore be considered merely as useful guidelines for achieving good organizational structure. Hardly a management system of any complexity now exists which does not violate one or more of these principles on occasion, sometimes with sound justification; nevertheless, these principles are useful, and careful consideration should be given to the wisdom and consequences of violating any one of them before the action is taken.

Principle 1: Scalar Principle. This principle states that authority and responsibility should flow smoothly in an unbroken chain from the chief executive to the lowest organizational levels. In effect, it establishes the organization as a hierarchy of authority/responsibility roles, with each employee cognizant of his role in the hierarchy. Transgressions of the principle sometimes occur when an executive, seeking to gain visibility and power, attempts to undermine the authority of his superior by sidestepping him and coordinating directly with higher executives. Other instances involve the "empire builder" who eschews established organizational centers of responsibility in order to create additional responsibilities for the activities under his own control. Violations of the scalar principle are usually considered disruptive to the orderly exercise of responsibilities within an organization.

Principle 2: Unity of Command. This principle requires that no member of an organization should report to more than one superior on any given aspect of his job. The principle is central to the concept of command. In practice, the close interplay among line and staff roles in a functional organization sometimes requires that an employee be responsible to several persons in fulfilling his total job requirements. This is acceptable practice provided the employee's superiors do not have overlapping authority over any set of common tasks, thus creating the possibility of conflicting directives with respect to a given task.

When this principle is violated it often has serious consequences, eventually if not immediately; for authority is undermined, discipline is in jeopardy, order is disturbed, and stability is threatened.[2] Deviations from the unity-of-command principle may arise from any of several sources: imperfect delineation of departmental responsibilities, divided employee activities, a supervisor preempting the authority of an employee's legitimate superior to gain time or power, and so forth. These and similar conditions should be examined carefully to prevent the erosion of good management through unintentional dual-authority situations.*

Principle 3: Exception Principle. The concept of a management hierarchy suggests that decisions of a similar or recurring character should be made routinely at the lower levels of management, while unusual decisions are made at higher levels. This principle of exception allows for a smooth consistency in the decision-making affairs of the organization. It provides the relatively inexperienced manager with a training base where he can improve his management skills through decision-making powers which are consistent with his experience. Moreover, it frees the more experienced executives to make the difficult decisions involving unusual or unprecedented problems that have broader implications for the organization.

President Harry S. Truman had a plaque on his desk in the White House inscribed "The buck stops here." This sign symbolizes the chief executive's responsibility to make those decisions which cannot be delegated or which are passed up the chain of command by personnel who lacked the authority to make such judgments. The principle of exception should be applied at all management levels to ensure that a balance is maintained between infrequent and unique decisions made by higher executives and routine decisions made among the more numerous management personnel at lower levels. Failure to strike this proper balance can overtax key executives and create conditions that breed decisions of poor quality.

* The section "Matrix Organization" describes one organizational structure wherein the unity-of-command principle is deliberately discarded for a dual-authority system. As brought out there, however, there are considerable difficulties in regulating a dual-authority system so as to maintain a proper balance of power.

Principle 4: Span of Control. It is generally accepted that there is a small fixed number of persons that a manager can supervise effectively. This number depends on the skill and experience of the manager and on where he stands in the organizational hierarchy. Whatever this number may be, however, if exceeded it will tend to dilute the quality of supervision exercised in the organization, or infringe on the time the manager would otherwise use to attend to his nonadministrative responsibilities. Since the manager has a finite amount of time and energy to devote to his job, the number of persons he can properly supervise cannot be increased beyond a certain point without incurring a sacrifice somewhere.

It is difficult to place a numerical value on span of control which has any real meaning across a spectrum of management responsibilities. The span of control can be larger at the lower levels of the organization, where supervision tends to be of a clear-cut, routine nature; however, near the top, where the decisions are more unique and wide-ranging, the span of control is usually smaller, as more time must be given to coordinate the activities of the senior executive and those reporting to him.

Principle 5: Short Chain of Command. This principle holds that the number of distinct management levels in the hierarchical chain of command should be kept as small as possible. The phrase "as small as possible" is clearly a relative one, for the number of management levels tends to increase as the number of employees increases. Nevertheless, this principle should be used as a general guideline by all organizations to maintain accurate communication and quick response time to directives.

The principles of span of control and short chain of command can be related in an approximate way to the number of employees in an organization. Let S be the span of control, a number assumed to be the same for each manager in the organization, and let L be the number of distinct management levels from the chief executive down to the lowest level of management. The number of managerial employees is then approximately

$$N_m = \sum_{n=1}^{L} S^{n-1}$$

and the total number of employees is about

$$N_t = \sum_{n=1}^{L+1} S^{n-1} *$$

The implications of this simple calculation are given in Figure 2-1, which shows how the number of managerial employees is related to span of control and the number of management levels. Each level of management added to an organization permits accommodation of a vastly greater number of employees, many more than can be provided by adding an additional number to the average span of control. If a company of fixed size were to add one more level of management, the average span of control would have to be cut back substantially. This situation could conceivably create a less challenging and less efficient management environment.

Principle 6: Departmentalization. This principle deals with the way in which an organization or institution is broken down into distinct administrative units and coordinated both vertically and horizontally. There is no optimal way of achieving such a structure for all organizations, since each organization has its own special characteristics which favor one approach or another.

The general problem is to create a departmentalized structure in such a way as to minimize the total cost of achieving the organization goals. This problem is often approached by grouping activities according to either commonality of skills employed (technical, informational, equipment, and so forth) or commonality of purpose or mission. Departmentalization by skills usually is more favorable for smaller organizations, which can better capitalize on the potential for economy through specialization; for larger organizational structures, however, where coordination costs can become very significant, departmentalization through commonality of purpose is usually more efficient.[3]

These two approaches to departmentalization—by skills employed and by purposes shared—present a problem in tradeoff between the gains achieved through specialization and those

---

* Assuming, for simplicity, that all nonmanagerial personnel occupy the level below the lowest management level.

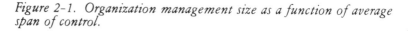

Figure 2-1. Organization management size as a function of average span of control.

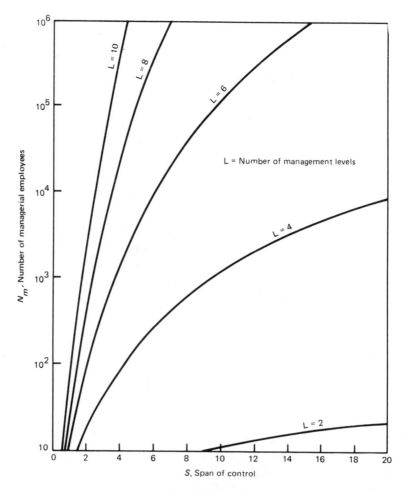

gained through coordination. Any sound departmentalization plan must certainly examine the nature of the working relationships between closely connected activities. Competition between administrative units, for example, can be an asset to an organization if competitive efforts are channeled constructively toward organization goals, and if no excess competition is encouraged which may create undesirable internal frictions. Also, when it is difficult to differentiate the separate responsibilities of two or more units, these units should be consolidated or departmentalized in a manner that will clarify lines of responsibility.

In addition to the two common approaches for departmentalization just mentioned, others can be used in their place (or sometimes in conjunction with them) to suit special organizational purposes. Departmentalization by location, for example, is useful in the distribution of goods or services throughout a variety of geographic regions. Still another approach to departmentalization is by clientele, for example, wholesale and retail, or government and industrial. Regardless of the approach taken, however, the objective of departmentalization must be the most cost-effective structure possible in pursuit of stated organization goals. This key concept, although it may appear simple, is manifestly complex to implement across all administrative units of the organization. It has defied many attempts to model the problem of departmentalization quantitatively, chiefly because of the complex behavioral patterns of employees within the organization.

Principle 7: Balance. Of all the basic organizational principles, balance is perhaps the most difficult to define and achieve, because it is so highly subjective. Balance has to do with determining the size of the administrative units within the organization so that they will be geared to equivalent production capacities. This concept is most easily implemented in a production-oriented organization whose activities constitute a more or less constant flow process. Then, the size of each unit can be adjusted in terms of space, personnel, inventory, and budget to a common level of operations. In other kinds of organizations, however, where the work is nonrepetitive or nonroutine and where the workload can vary considerably overall and within the administrative units, balance is much more difficult to achieve. This is particularly true within high-technology organizations, which are among the most ill suited to precise planning.

On a larger scale, balance concerns the overall organizational structure as well as the size of the administrative units. There usually will be an ideal balance between average span of control and the number of managerial levels in an organization. (See

Figure 2-1.) This balance most often comes about through a slow evolutionary process rather than through deliberate analytical planning.

Principle 8: Decentralization. Decentralization refers to the organizational philosophy of placing decision-making processes at lower administrative levels. It is thus closely linked to the exception principle and the concept of delegation of authority. Decentralization is not an organizational paradigm toward which all should strive; there are cases, however, where it is especially desirable. It is particularly attractive where speed in decision making is important, so that authority for making firm decisions is vested in those managers who are most approachable and most closely connected to the problem at hand.

Decentralization is also ideally suited to large organizations, where the base of decision-making authority should be broad, as well as to organizations of moderate size which are rich in technical and decision-making talent. R. J. Cordiner, in describing the General Electric Company's successful experience with decentralization, has suggested the following list of ten guiding principles for effective decentralization.[4]

> Decentralization places authority to make decisions at points as near as possible to where actions take place.
>
> Decentralization is likely to get best overall results by getting the greatest and most directly applicable knowledge and the most timely understanding actually into play on the greatest number of decisions.
>
> Decentralization will work if real authority is delegated; and not if details then have to be reported, or, worse yet, if they have to be "checked" first.
>
> Decentralization requires confidence that associates in decentralized positions will have the capacity to make sound decisions in the majority of cases—and such confidence starts at the executive level. Unless the president and all the other officers have a deep personal conviction and an active desire to decentralize full decision-making responsibility and authority, actual decentralization will never take place. The officers must set an example in the art of full delegation.
>
> Decentralization requires understanding that the main role of staff or services is the rendering of assistance and advice to line

operators through a relatively few experienced people, so that those making decisions can themselves make them correctly.

Decentralization requires realization that the natural aggregate of many individually sound decisions will be better for the business and for the public than centrally planned and controlled decisions.

Decentralization rests on the need to have general business objectives, organization structure, relationships, policies, and measurements known, understood, and followed; but realizing that definition of policies does not necessarily mean uniformity of methods of executing such policies in decentralized operations.

Decentralization can be achieved only when higher executives realize that authority genuinely delegated to lower echelons cannot, in fact, also be retained by them. We have, today, officers and managers who still believe in decentralization down to themselves and no further. By paying lip-service to decentralization, but actually reviewing detailed work and decisions and continually "second-guessing" their associates, such officers keep their organization in confusion and prevent the growth of self-reliant men.

Decentralization will work only if responsibility commensurate with decision-making authority is truly accepted and exercised at all levels.

Decentralization requires personnel policies based on measured performance, enforced standards, rewards for good performance, and removal for incapacity or poor performance.

The Bureaucratic Structure

The eight basic principles of management combine to make up the essence of what Max Weber originally termed a *bureaucracy*.* A bureaucratic structure is designed to foster an impersonal and rational orientation toward task accomplishment which is conducive to efficient administration. Contrary to the opprobrious popular impression, well-run bureaucratic structure is the cornerstone of modern organization. The essential elements of a bureaucratic structure as presented by Weber are:

—Required organizational activities are distributed as official duties.
—The organization is arranged as a hierarchy of offices, with each office under the control and supervision of the next highest.
—Operations are governed by a consistent set of rules and policies.

* See, specifically, his *Theory of Social and Economic Organization*, published in 1922, two years following his death.

—Employees are appointed (not elected) on the basis of their technical qualifications, and are not subject to arbitrary termination.
—A system of promotions exists according to which an employee may advance by virtue of seniority, achievement, or both.
—Employees are subject to strict and systematic discipline and control in the conduct of their impersonal official duties.

As can be seen, there is a close connection between Weber's elements of bureaucracy and the basic principles of management discussed earlier. Despite attacks by Weber's critics that he is too autocratic, his model of bureaucratic structure has had profound impact on contemporary organizational thought.

LINE, STAFF, AND FUNCTIONAL STRUCTURES

Most organizational systems contain three reasonably distinct modes of operation through which all employees contribute their efforts. These are commonly known as line, staff, and functional organizational systems and are associated with the degree of responsibility the employee assumes for the end product while carrying out his duties. An understanding of the nature of and the distinctions among these systems and how they are orchestrated in an organization is of basic importance in grasping the significance of organizational structure.

Line organization is the oldest and simplest form of organizational structure. Here, employees in the vertical reporting chain of command all contribute directly to the production of the organization's basic products or operations. That is, in a pure line organization each employee's contribution is related in some direct manner to the organization's output. The line supervisor has the responsibility and authority over those reporting directly to him to take whatever action is reasonably indicated to fulfill his unit's obligations as related to output. This kind of direct authority, flowing from the top to the bottom in the organization in keeping with the scalar principle, characterizes the line structure.

The *staff organization* adds a second dimension to the overall structure by providing support and advisory roles. No organization of any size or complexity can be viable over the long term without making provisions for these specialized staff services which, although vitally important, are related only indirectly to the ultimate product line or operations. The staff organization is characterized by its lack of authority over the line operations. Its purpose is to provide line management with the specialized data and counsel needed for decision making and for the control of line operations.

In many kinds of modern organizations, certain positions— indeed even entire departments—require the flexibility to blend staff responsibilities with limited line authority in enforcing directives in certain well-defined areas. Such positions possess what is termed *functional authority*. As usually applied, the functional role is ascribed to the staff worker or manager who has some limited and specific authority bearing directly on operations. For example, in an R&D organization the legal department, a staff unit, may be given authority to reject patent applications approved by line departments. The personnel department may be given specific responsibilities and authorities over line unit hiring practices commensurate with existing federal hiring and antidiscrimination regulations. At times, the term functional authority may refer to the line manager. For example, the vice-president of engineering may be given functional authority over his R&D directors in matters concerning the scheduling of production jobs.

The distinction between line, staff, and functional authority is sometimes a fuzzy one in practice, although it is in the best interests of management to delineate responsibilities to clarify authority roles. Furthermore, what may be a line function in one organization may be a staff function in another, making it impossible to classify line/staff roles by profession. For example, the research department would certainly carry line authority in an R&D organization, but may be a limited staff function in a highly product-oriented concern. Not infrequently, an executive may exercise line, staff, and functional authorities interchangeably in carrying out his day-to-day responsibilities. For example, the director of accounting may administer the activities of his unit (line) and furnish cost-accounting data to line directors (staff), while at the same time managing the development of improved payroll procedures for the entire organization (functional). Whether such a person is classified as line, staff, or functional depends on what he is doing at the moment.

In common parlance, the term *functional* is also used loosely to describe a total organizational structure composed of line, staff, and functional roles. The terms *functional authority* and *functional organization* thus have distinct meanings, although they are sometimes confused and incorrectly applied.

Few modern organizations of any complexity, especially those involved in R&D, can operate as strictly line organizations. What is needed is a blend of all three types of organizational authority structures as in the functional organization, where they are tightly integrated and combined in the proper proportions to meet established objectives in the most efficient manner. In designing the organization it is important to have a clear understanding of the relative strengths and weaknesses of the line, staff, and functional systems so that the optimum blend can be found. The relative advantages of each has been summarized by Massie.[5] (See Table 2-1.) The advantages of one system tend to be the disadvantages of another, particularly in the case of line and staff structures.

Table 2-1. Comparison of line and staff organizational structures.

	ADVANTAGES	DISADVANTAGES
Line	Maintains simplicity Makes clear division of authority Encourages speedy action	Neglects specialists in planning Overworks key men Depends upon retention of a few key men
Staff	Enables specialists to give expert advice Frees the line executive of detailed analysis Affords young specialists a means of training	Confuses organization if functions are not clear Reduces power of experts to place recommendations into action Tends toward centralization of organization

SOURCE: J. L. Massie, *Essentials of Management,* 2d ed. Englewood Cliffs, N.J.: Prentice-Hall, 1971.

An effective manager is quick to appreciate the need for building good cooperation among line and staff personnel. He also recognizes the latent sources of friction that can destroy such cooperation and impair operations. Line personnel may tend to view staff personnel as organizational glut—not only who fail to contribute their share of direct costs (i.e., they are carried as overhead) but who presume to interfere with line operations by giving advice/recommendations when not called upon to do so. Also, staff personnel often have a direct line of communication with the higher levels of line management, and this sometimes creates envy and frustration in the lower line manager who usually does not have such rapport with higher management.

On the opposite side, staff personnel frequently feel thwarted by lack of the authority that in their view should go hand in hand with an advisory position. There is a tendency for staff at times to view line managers as unimaginative functionaries who enjoy the power but shun informed counsel.

In practice, of course, staff departments often have functional authority and hence can exercise limited authority. Functional authority in staff departments provides the organization with the flexibility needed to relieve line executives of routine decision-making responsibilities and to obviate the need for exceptionally well-rounded executives. Functional authority, however, does complicate organizational relationships. In particular, the need to place limits on the authority of staff employees can create coordination and communication problems.

ORGANIZATION DESIGN

It is common practice to represent the structure of an organization graphically by means of an organization chart. This chart is a schematic representation which may be used to define not only the structure of the organization but also the reporting relationships, the flow of work, and the areas of responsibility within the enterprise. Its purpose is twofold. First, it gives outsiders (suppliers, clients, investors, and the interested public) an integrated view of the working elements of the organization. Second, it serves to identify for the employees the levels of authority, the reporting chain, and in general the detailed anatomy of the company. The organization chart describes the formal organizational structure, but seldom the project management structure, and never the informal structure. Because the organization is a constantly changing entity, with contractions and expansions, with employees joining and leaving, with promotions and other job changes, and with shifting responsibilities, the organization chart is always subject to rapid obsolescence. To be of value the chart must be constantly updated to reflect these changes.

The organization chart is composed of a series of blocks which identify the major positions or activities of the organization. These blocks are connected vertically and laterally to define the hierarchy and span of operations. In addition to identifying positions, the organizational blocks may identify the person responsible for the function and/or may describe the functional responsibility. Figure 2-2 shows three possibilities.

The arrangement of the organizational blocks indicates the structure of the organization. Blocks that are coordinated vertically down from the chief executive usually indicate line activities, whereas staff functions are often represented by blocks placed laterally and not directly connected to another block. Figure 2-3 shows the structure of a typical functional organization composed of line and staff operations.

In addition to describing the structure of the organization, the organization chart reveals something of its nature and its stage in the life cycle. Structures which are relatively flat, with little vertical depth, may indicate a decentralized organization with short chains of command and in which the major units function as relatively autonomous profit centers under direct control of the chief executive. Such shallow charts are characteristic of retail businesses and conglomerate organizations. On the other hand, shallow charts are indicative also of organizations which are in the initial, or growth, stage of the life cycle (see "The Marketing Function" in Chapter 4). Here, the basic functional areas are spread laterally but are not yet developed in depth through growth and specialization. Such a chart is shown in Figure 2-4. At this early stage in an organization's growth, the head of each department is likely to have a broader scope of responsibility

Figure 2-2. Functional identifications used in organizational blocks.

Director of Marketing

Director of marketing
Ralph A. Davison

Director of marketing
(domestic sales, marketing research)

Figure 2-3. Arrangement of line (shaded) and staff (unshaded) functions on a typical organization chart.

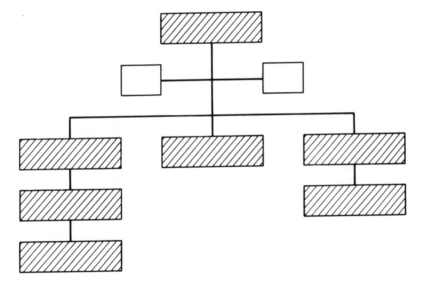

than he would have in a mature organization in which functional areas are more specialized.

As the organization grows toward maturity, the principal functional areas expand and divide and tend to develop more levels of management responsibility under their senior executives. Along with its vertical growth, the organization will usually grow laterally, increasing the direct span of control of the chief

Figure 2-4. A shallow organization chart, characteristic of a young and/or decentralized organization.

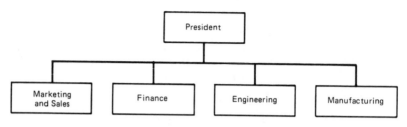

Figure 2-5. Organization chart showing the organization represented by Figure 2-4 in a later stage of maturity.

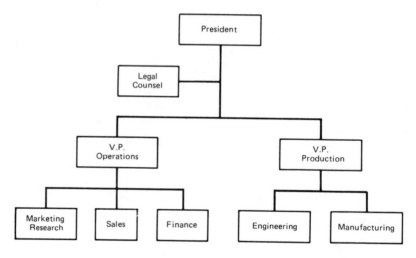

executive. This growth in the number and layers of functional areas breeds a more structured system of titles, which are then introduced into the organizational blocks. Such a title structure serves not only to establish a reporting hierarchy but also to provide status. Figure 2-5 shows a later stage in the development of the organization depicted in Figure 2-4.

In the later growth stages of a large organization, the functional structure may become too complex to be represented in a single chart. A master organization chart is then used to display the major divisions, and secondary charts are developed to show the detailed divisional and departmental anatomy. These secondary organization charts usually include the name and title of all members of the unit's staff. Because of normal growth and turnover in each functional unit, these charts tend toward obsolescence much more rapidly than the master chart does, and they must be updated more frequently.

PROJECT ORGANIZATION

The project organization concept emerged in the aerospace industry in the 1950s. The rapid growth in technology created a demand for the management of ad hoc projects—well-defined activities which, over relatively short periods of time, required the participation of numerous skilled specialists. Such programs, particularly those requiring the development of new technology, were ill suited to the traditional functional organizational structure because the traditional organization was designed for ongoing and repetitious activities. Project management developed rapidly, taking on several forms designed to cope with the needs of various kinds of projects. Today, the concept of project management pervades high technology in all government, private, and corporate sectors, and is being found increasingly in certain specialized but nontechnical areas of commercial enterprise.

Basic Elements

The project organization is a form of management designed to accomplish a specified set of objectives which characterize the project. Projects differ widely in size and scope, but all share three common requirements: to meet specified technical objectives, to meet them within a given target date, and to meet them within the project budget. These requirements are all set forth in a legally binding contract.* The project management must draw together the appropriate technical and support personnel from within the organization, and this project team works collectively toward the goal of project completion, and hence toward obsolescence.

* Exceptions occur in the case of in-house or internally funded projects, where the project work agreement does not carry legal authority.

A single person—the project or program manager—is usually the chief executive of the project. Ultimately, all responsibility for successfully meeting the program objectives resides with the project manager. In order that he may fulfill these responsibilities he should be accorded full authority over all program activities. The project manager's responsibilities include all those traditionally associated with line management: planning, organizing, directing, and controlling. In conjunction with his entire project team, he must function as an organization within the context of the parent organization. It is this juxtaposition of one organizational form with another that creates special challenges and problems for the project manager.

Figure 2-6 illustrates the organizational structure of several projects within a research and development department. In its pure form, the total effort of this department encompasses a number of projects. Note that in the structure shown in the figure the project manager has no formal reporting or coordinating channel with the various other department heads (Production, Marketing, and so forth). In structuring the project itself, the overall activity may be broken down into various task elements, for each of which a task leader is appointed (as depicted in the figure), or the project may be organized along functional lines, such as engineering, production, quality control, and so forth.

Working within his host or parent organization, the project manager assembles his project team from the available pool of line, staff, and functional employees. Occasionally, a large project will require that new employees—permanent or temporary—be brought into the organization to be assigned to that project. Nevertheless, the project team size, which is related directly to the project size and indirectly to the period of performance, must be small relative to the size of the parent organization. Otherwise, the functional base of technical skills and facilities would not be sufficient to provide the project team with the personnel it needs.

The project management concept offers several advantages over the traditional functional management structure for finite, one-of-a-kind projects. The advantages of project management which loom as most important are these:

Figure 2-6. *Typical project organizational structure.*

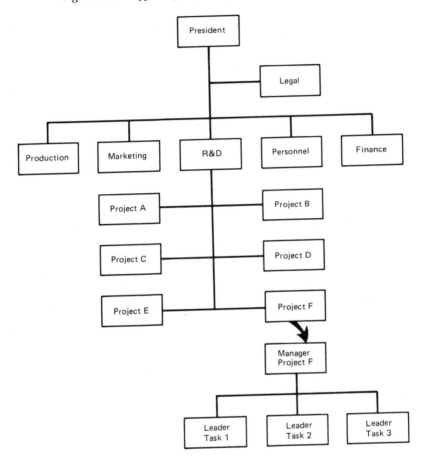

—Makes more effective use of skilled technical specialists.
—Provides for an interchange of ideas among diverse technical specialists (the wheel is not constantly reinvented).
—May command full-time attention of personnel.
—Provides challenging and unique management opportunities for lower and middle management.
—Establishes an identity or focal point for an activity which is more visible to customers and the public.
—Is results-oriented.

Project management is not without its disadvantages, of course. Most of its shortcomings stem from the limits placed on the project manager's authority by the senior management of the parent organization; some aspects will be considered later.

The Project Manager

The size of the project, in terms of budget and staff, has an important influence on the day-to-day activities of the project manager. At one end of the scale, a small research program may be staffed by only the project manager himself—and then perhaps only part-time. In this case the project manager has very few administrative duties, and most of his project time is concerned with technical activities. At the other end of the scale a large program, say on the order of $1 million or more per year, may have its own administrative staff, responsible to the project manager, to handle such matters as scheduling and interface requirements, assembly, production, reporting and client relations, and the like. Here, the project manager's time is almost wholly consumed with administrative matters.

Each project manager must function somewhere within this broad spectrum on every program. The degree of managerial experience and competency required of him, however, will depend on how deeply he is involved in administrative matters—that is, on the size of the program. His training ground is his organization. To be effective in managing large programs he must be familiar with all facets of the organization, technical and nontechnical, and must have experience in the management of smaller programs. In recognition of the key responsibilities discharged by their project managers in handling large programs, some organizations elevate the status of such a position by title and compensation. The project management position thus becomes a professional position unto itself, requiring both general management and technical skills.

The managerial climate in which the project manager works makes his job difficult and complex. Not only are his responsibilities numerous and varied, but his role as manager of a temporary organizational system within a permanent organizational structure requires exceptional tact, persuasive capabilities, and

dedication. Figure 2-7 outlines the major administrative responsibilities of the project manager. These responsibilities encompass all the requirements placed on the manager of a large project; small projects often involve far less in the way of formal
planning and controlling.

Figure 2-7. The project manager's administrative responsibilities.

DEFINING THE PROGRAM

    Life cycle estimates
    Work statement breakdown
    Resource needs and allocations

DEVELOPING THE PROGRAM TEAM

    Definition of staff requirements
    Filling staff needs by negotiation with line managers
    Scheduling and interfacing team members' participation

DEVELOPING THE PROGRAM PLAN

    Time planning and scheduling
    Selecting the appropriate planning tools
    Developing program schedules and reporting procedures

IMPLEMENTING THE PROGRAM PLAN

    Opening channels of communication
    Developing sources of input data
    Preparing a documentation plan

PROGRAM CONTROL

    Cost control techniques
    Project life cycles
    Liaison with client and subcontractors
    Establishing a milestone control plan
    Network scheduling analysis and updating

Although most of the project manager's activities are intraprogram in nature, that is, conducted within the program team, some
of his responsibilities are interorganizational in character. This is
particularly true in the planning aspects of the program, although

the project manager's functions may interface with other operating and staff functions of the organization in other program phases. It is frequently these interorganizational activities that create the most difficult problems for the project manager. In developing his program staff, for example, the project manager must borrow from the operating divisions (profit centers) those persons who will fulfill the program's required mix of technical expertise. However, he may lack the administrative authority to pull people from line departments and place them on a project. Thus, he is put in the position of having to negotiate with line (and staff) managers to meet his staffing requirements. The effective project manager must therefore develop a good working rapport with the functional managers to accomplish these objectives.

The role of the project manager is quite distinct from that of the engineer or scientist who is placed on the program team. Unlike any other team member (whose technical background he may share), the project manager must be a synergist within the organization, communicating and coordinating both vertically and laterally. His dual responsibilities for technical and administrative matters require that he possess credible skills in both areas: the project manager who is deficient in either area cannot be totally effective in administering his program. Although he should be capable of performing detailed analysis independently, his role as project manager generally precludes it. The role of the project manager has been described as directed toward professional supervisor-employee relationships, independence of thought, dependence on the creative talents of subordinates, willingness to sanction the power of subordinates (colleague authority), and a strong emphasis on subordinate norms and needs. Whereas most supervisors of nontechnical activities (e.g., manufacturing) have an upward orientation in coordinating ideas and activities, the project manager relies more on downward and lateral input.

The characteristics of a good project manager have been summed up by his abilities to communicate, regulate, negotiate, and motivate. Smith[6] has described the substance of *communication* in the project management context as:

—Checking to see that instructions are being carried out.
—Keeping key people informed, through formal and informal meetings, distribution lists, and so forth.
—Listening to and understanding another's viewpoint.
—Maintaining personal contact with the project team.
—Being constructive (positive) rather than critical (negative).
—Explaining the reasons for decisions to those who will be influenced.

Regulation refers to the budgeting of effort and capital among the various project activities, and adjusting as required to meet program objectives. The proposal provides the basis for the regulation function, but it usually must be developed in greater depth and detail if it is to serve as a control standard against which performance is to be compared. Each budgeted task should be described in sufficient detail so that all concerned know what is to be done, how, and by whom. Task definitions can be formalized through a task assignment form similar to the one shown in Figure 2-8. The project manager uses this information in connection with his cost data in an active control mode, continuously comparing planned and actual performance and adjusting activities to keep the two consistent.

Negotiation is the art of bargaining to reach a mutually acceptable settlement. The project manager is frequently involved in negotiation, and the adept project manager hones this skill to a fine edge. Negotiation is usually first encountered when the last details of the pending contract are settled. The negotiations may revolve around setting contract costs after the proposal has been technically accepted, or may concern the process of competitive negotiation to win a contract award. In either case, the program task elements and associated costs must be defended and negotiated, often in minute detail. In the case of the pending contract the emphasis is on cost, since the technical effort has already been defined. In competitive negotiations the emphasis shifts to the technical requirements, although task costs are of vital interest too.

After the contract is awarded, the project manager still finds himself in a negotiating position. He must work out suitable staffing arrangements for his project with line managers, in effect bargaining with them for services. He may also have to make arrangements with the organization's staff functions to supply the

Figure 2-8. *Task assignment form.*

Program Title _____

Task Title   _____ Charge No. _____

Task Leader _____   _____
                  Accepted by   Date

Group or Dept. _____   _____
              Supervisor Approval   Date

Program Manager _____   _____
                Authorized by   Date

TASK:

Scheduled Start _____ Duration of Effort _____

Description _____

_____

_____

_____

_____

End Requirements _____

_____

_____

BUDGET:

   Labor   Hours   Other Direct (material, travel)

_____ _____   _____

_____ _____   _____

_____ _____   _____

WORK PACKAGE COMPLETED:

Hours Expended _____ Date Completed _____

accounting and other pertinent program data. As the program progresses, the sponsor may request redirections or changes in the technical effort (scope) as given in the original work statement. However trivial the case may appear, the project manager should never agree to a change of scope commitment without consulting with his contracting officer concerning the possible cost and contractual implications. In his relations with his client, the project manager must tactfully negotiate such requested changes so as not to give offense, yet he must protect himself from cost liabilities.

In addition to the qualities described above, the effective project manager must be able to *motivate* his team, since the project's ultimate performance is heavily dependent on collective motivation. (Much more is said concerning motivation in Chapter 3.) Each employee is subject to leadership and motivation, and it is the responsibility of the project manager to find the key to motivating each project member. Some ways that have proved successful in motivating project team members are:

—By example—the project manager should cultivate the same degree of visibility and reputation for staying with the job as he expects of his team members.
—By adopting a positive attitude—avoiding discussions that are critical of other persons or groups within the organization.
—By being optimistic—and communicating an attitude of successfully coping with changing requirements.
—By keeping all promises and commitments that are made, and not making those that cannot be kept.
—By distributing customer contact information and specification changes to all technical persons affected.
—By giving each project member the attention he requires—this depends not only on the nature of the assignment, but also on the degree of independence the member prefers.

The project manager's role in the organization is admittedly difficult. His assignment, by definition, is temporary. It is, moreover, fraught with the uncertainties which stem from the possibilities of cutbacks and cancellation and from the caprice of the political environment that provides the program's funding. Unlike the case of technology development, these are external factors over which the project manager has essentially no control.

Compounding this uncertain environment are interorganizational conflicts which bear directly on program management but yet are not subject to the project manager's control. He seldom has full authority over the functional units of the organization that complement his management needs, particularly those from separate departments or profit centers. Lacking this administrative authority, he must frequently make compromises in drawing functional support for the program. His program control responsibilities may have to be sacrificed if the organizational staff units (such as personnel, purchasing, accounting, and editorial) cannot (or will not) be responsive to his program needs.

Successful program completion is also predicated on the availability of physical resources, such as office, laboratory, and manufacturing space, equipment, and materials. To a large extent access to these resources is restricted by organizational considerations that the project manager cannot change. Again, he must rely on his persuasive powers and personal influence to do the best he can for his program within the given constraints. Finally, he is subject to control by his superior, and that control may at times have bearing on the program.

Thamhain and Wilemon[7] have examined sources of conflict between a project manager and those within the organization with whom he must interact during the project life cycle. Figure 2-9 shows one of the main results of their study, a ranking by intensity of the major sources of conflict involved in project management. The three areas of disagreement most likely to cause problems for the project manager are those over schedules, project priorities, and manpower resources. One reason why these issues may lead to the most intense conflicts is that their resolution lies in part with the functional support departments, over which the project manager has little or no control. Table 2-2 lists suggestions offered by Thamhain and Wilemon for recognizing and coping with conflict as it is likely to appear at various stages of the project life cycle.

The specific mode for addressing a conflict encounter will vary with the project manager and his perception of the gravity of the situation. Blake and Mouton[8] have delineated five distinct modes for handling conflict:

Figure 2-9. Mean conflict intensity profile over project life cycle.

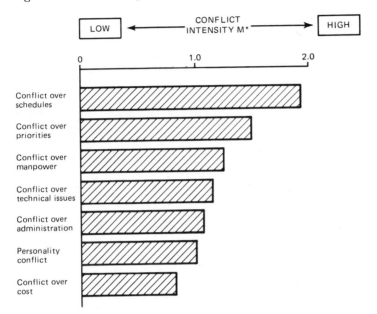

*M is the relative intensity of conflict perceived by project managers, measured on a four-point scale, 0-1-2-3, and averaged over the five sources: (1) conflict with functional departments, (2) conflict with assigned personnel, (3) conflict between team members, (4) conflict with superiors, and (5) conflict with subordinates. Hence it follows that $0 \leqslant M \leqslant 3$.

SOURCE: H.J. Thamhain and D.L. Wilemon, ''Conflict Management in Project Life Cycles,'' *Sloan Management Review*, Spring 1975. Reprinted with permission.

—Confrontation—directly facing conflicts which involve a problem-solving approach whereby affected parties work through their disagreements.

—Forcing—exerting one's own viewpoint at the potential expense of another's. Often characterized by competitiveness and a win/lose situation.

—Compromising—searching and bargaining for solutions which bring some degree of satisfaction to the parties in a dispute. Characterized by a give-and-take attitude.

—Smoothing—deemphasizing or avoiding areas of difference and emphasizing areas of agreement.

—Withdrawal—retreating or withdrawing from an actual or potential disagreement.

Table 2-2. Major sources of conflict throughout project life cycle.

PROJECT LIFE CYCLE PHASE	SOURCE OF CONFLICT	RECOMMENDATIONS FOR MINIMIZING DYSFUNCTIONAL CONSEQUENCES
Conceptual	**Priorities**	— Clearly defined plans. Joint decision making and/or consultation with affected parties.
		— Stress importance of project to goals of the organization.
	Procedures	— Develop detailed administrative operating procedures to be followed in conduct of project. Secure approval from key administrators. Develop statement of understanding or charter.
	Schedules	— Develop schedule commitments in advance of actual project commencement.
		— Forecast other departmental priorities and possible impact on project.
Initiation	**Priorities**	— Provide effective feedback to support areas on forecasted project plans and needs via status review sessions.
	Schedules	— Carefully schedule work breakdown packages (project subunits) in cooperation with functional groups.
	Procedures	— Contingency planning on key administrative issues.

Operational	Schedules	— Continually monitor work in progress. Communicate results to affected parties.
		— Forecast potential problems and consider alternatives.
		— Identify potential "trouble spots" needing closer surveillance.
	Technical	— Early resolution of technical problems.
		— Communication of schedule and budget restraints to technical personnel.
		— Emphasize adequate, early technical testing.
		— Facilitate early agreement on final designs.
	Manpower	— Forecast and communicate manpower requirements early.
		—Establish manpower requirements and priorities with functional and staff groups.
Terminal	Schedules	— Close monitoring of schedules throughout project life cycle.
		— Consider reallocation of available manpower to critical project areas prone to schedule slippages.
		— Attain prompt resolution of technical issues which may impact schedules.
	Personality and manpower	— Develop plans for reallocation of manpower upon project completion.
		— Maintain harmonious working relationships with project team and support groups. Try to loosen up "high-stress" environment.

SOURCE: H. J. Thamhain and D. L. Wilemon, "Conflict Management in Project Life Cycles," *Sloan Management Review*, Spring 1975. Reprinted with permission.

The confrontation and compromising approaches are the most commonly used, and are often the most effective.

The project management function is thus seen as both difficult and complex—demanding technical and administrative skills and subject to many constraints on the project manager's authority. Moreover, successful project management offers fewer visible rewards than technical performance does. The project manager often cannot afford the personal commitment of time required to achieve technical excellence—he must delegate this role to members of the project team. Because of this, he often finds it difficult to publish the results of his efforts, and tends to lose visibility among colleagues outside his organization. There are other kinds of rewards, however. The project manager's role in the organization continually changes as one project terminates and another begins. He has an intimate association with a whole project, from inception to completion, not merely a narrow slice of technology. Furthermore, what the project manager lacks in external visibility he makes up in internal visibility—he occupies a key position in the organization.

Dimensions of Project Management

One way to measure the dimensions of project management is to analyze the *project life cycle*. The life cycle concept is of basic importance in microeconomic theory (see Chapter 4), and adapting it to the R&D project is useful in understanding project management requirements. Karger and Murdick[9] have described the project life cycle in terms of four successive phases: conceptual, project initiation, operational, and terminal.

The *conceptual phase* consists of all preproposal activity, up to the time that a formal proposal is submitted. The proposal may be submitted to in-house management in quest of internal research and development (IR&D) support. Far more commonly, however, the proposal is submitted to an outside client or sponsoring agency, and may or may not be solicited by the client or agency.

The conceptual phase consists basically of problem definition and solution feasibility. This phase may develop in any of several ways. A problem and possible solution may be defined by the organization (government or commercial) that has the requirement. Once this is done that organization may initiate technical discussions with a chosen contractor, and these may then lead to a proposal and contract negotiations. Alternatively (and more commonly among organizations of the federal government), the sponsoring agency may solicit from the broad spectrum of qualified contractors for proposals aimed at the specified problem area. The conceptual phase may begin with the contractor, who perceives a technological problem and a solution approach and then attempts to interest certain organizations in sponsoring an R&D program.

Finally, in the case of large long-range programs, the customer may issue small feasibility study contracts to several competing contractors. Each contractor then develops his study, which forms the basis for a proposal for product development, and a single contractor is then selected for the ensuing major effort.

The *project initiation phase* begins with acceptance of the proposal, and involves the detailed program planning effort. The technical proposal usually lacks the depth of detail it would need to serve as a planning instrument, since it is prepared over a short period, often under great pressure. During the project initiation phase, program requirements are drawn up in detail, and project planning (including PERT and CPM models), organization, staffing, and control concepts are developed and key points of coordination are identified. Frequently this planning effort is facilitated by interaction with the sponsor, to clarify matters of technical procedure.

Following the project initiation phase, when all initial planning is complete, the *operational phase* begins. This phase spans all technical activities directed at fulfilling the work scope and producing the end product (report, prototype development, production hardware units, and so forth). During this phase the project manager is called on to exercise his best technical and administrative skills to lead the project successfully to conclusion.

Finally, the *terminal phase* begins at the close of the technical activity (as required by the program schedule) and brings the program to termination. This phase consists in consolidating information, massaging data, sifting and analyzing results, and drawing conclusions in preparation for the final report.

The program team is cut down to the few senior people needed to accomplish this task, and excess personnel must be reassigned to another project or elsewhere in the organization. Records must be prepared for storage, and arrangements for end-item deliverables must be made. Like the operational phase, the terminal phase places substantial administrative demands on the project manager as he strives to conclude the project on time and within cost forecasts. Every project, regardless of its original size, ultimately declines in size to one with a budget of 5 percent of the initial contract cost, and efficient management of that 5 percent is crucial to the financial performance of the program.

Figure 2-10 shows a typical project life cycle as composed of these four sequential phases. Many projects, of course, are terminated for various reasons before fulfilling their complete life cycles; this occurs most commonly in the conceptual phase. As suggested by Figure 2-10, the operational phase normally consumes the greatest portion of the project's labor and capital investment.

Each project has its own unique life cycle, to be developed over the life of the project by project management to suit the unique requirements of that project. Project managers should be sufficiently adaptive to adjust to shifting program requirements as the work progresses. Technical requirements may change in response to contractual modifications or unforeseen problems.

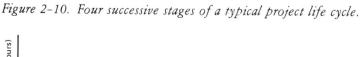

Figure 2-10. Four successive stages of a typical project life cycle.

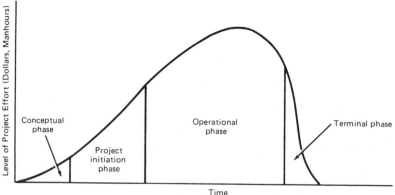

Points of coordination within the organization or with the sponsor may change. Scheduling problems caused by delayed inventory supplies or in-house work delays may require accelerated work efforts in certain areas. Effective and adaptive management must be exercised to cope with these problems as they arise.

A question of basic importance to program management deals with criteria for judging the success of the program. What yardsticks can be applied to individual projects, and how? Bennigson[10] proposes two sets of criteria, one of which measures project success, and the other, management success. Project success is associated directly with the end product, and may include time, cost, and performance. Other criteria, however, may also be applied, for example, follow-on work, internal spin-off benefits, and cultivation of sound customer relations. The important thing is to weigh all these criteria in relation to each other: a project which concludes with both cost and time overruns may be a smashing success if it opens up significant new markets and leads to follow-on work.

Management success deals with the selection of strategic management goals for evaluating management success. Bennigson proposes five such goals:

—Obtaining the commitment of the program team to the accomplishment of program goals.
—Achieving adequate coordination and collaboration.
—Making relevant status information visible.
—Satisfying the personal and job security needs of project personnel.
—Terminating the project appropriately, either by completion or by developing follow-on efforts.

All successful project management approaches must satisfy these goals, although their relative importance may vary from one program to another.

MATRIX ORGANIZATION

Deficiencies of Traditional Approaches

Earlier parts of this chapter have dealt with traditional functional organizational structures and the project management approach to R&D activities. Traditional organization theory is seen as developing around the basic principles of division of labor, scalar and functional processes, and structure. Division of labor concerns the way employees are partitioned into various groups within the organization. Scalar and functional processes relate, respectively, to the vertical and horizontal coordination and growth of the organization. Structure is that which binds the functions together in some kind of logical relationship. It defines the modes of coordination between functional areas and is designed to achieve work flow.

A number of integrating mechanisms are used to accomplish functional coordination. Among them are written policies and procedures, planning, and liaison groups to perform activities common to two or more departments. These and other mechanisms are used in an attempt to minimize a fundamental deficiency of the functional-type organization: the difficulty in coordinating the activities of the different profit centers within the structure to achieve timely and satisfactory completion within budgeted costs. Indeed, completing all projects simultaneously and on time—with appropriate quality, within budget costs, and with full utilization of all specialist resources—is a goal rarely achieved in the functional organization.

Because of this inherent deficiency of the functional organization, the project management approach developed within the R&D community to meet the special demands of high-technology projects. As has been shown, this organizational structure provides for close coordination across functional areas and is well suited to short-term projects requiring quick reaction capabilities. In addition, all responsibility and authority for quality, schedule, and cost performance is vested in a single individual. Despite these advantages, however, project management suffers from its inability to utilize the total pool of employees effectively. The problem is that of allocating human and capital resources in the most efficient manner throughout multiple project activities to maximize overall performance. If this is not achieved, wasteful duplication occurs, which ultimately imposes an unanticipated financial burden on the organization.

Thus, each form of organization, functional and project, has its own set of advantages and disadvantages. The problem is that when one form of organization is chosen, the strengths of the other form are forfeited. The choice of a specific organization design is closely connected to the question of whether project completion is more important than advanced technical development, that is, the basic objectives of the organization.

A New Approach

In the 1960s the aerospace industry, recognizing that both technical performance and coordination are important in R&D, began to experiment with organizational structures which would combine the advantages of both the functional and the project forms. The result of this evolutionary process is the matrix organizational structure, a form particularly suited to the needs of high-technology industry.

The term *matrix* derives from the two-dimensional structure of this organizational form. One dimension comprises the line or functional activities that provide the pool of support for the ongoing projects. Research, Systems Design, Production, and Business Operations are but some of the functional activities that may be called upon to support project activities. The other dimension of the matrix organization is made up of the programs themselves.* They may be many in number, and all have a relatively short life cycle; hence this dimension, in contrast to the fixed dimension of functional structure, is constantly changing.

An example of a typical matrix organizational structure is shown in Figure 2-11. The various functional units which contribute directly to program activities are arranged horizontally, while the programs themselves are arranged vertically. The intersection points, or nodes, characterize a particular functional unit's contribution to a particular program. This contribution may be measured in personnel (man-hours) directly assigned to that

* Here again the designation *program* is preferred over *project* in acknowledgment of the fact that several separate functional units are involved, and the total program effort tends to be relatively large.

Figure 2-11. A typical matrix organizational structure.

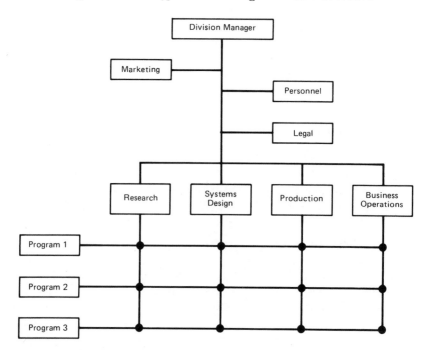

program for a specified period of time. On adding the manpower allocations at each node along a vertical column, the total contribution from that department or functional unit to all program activities is determined. This total must clearly be no greater than the total personnel pool attached to that department, or it will be overcommitting itself. Normally, the objective is to maintain the total near some given fraction of the functional unit's capacity, to provide an adequate pool for the ebb and flow of personnel to programs and allow nonprogram activities to be conducted.

By adding up the contributions in each node across any program row, the total personnel commitment to that program is established. Since the life cycle requirements of each program will impose varying staff demands on each functional unit at different stages of the program's life, the time commitments at each node in the matrix organization will change continuously. Because of this, each program requires continuous planning and updating if the matrix organization is to work effectively.

In order for the matrix organization to function effectively, management information from the program groups must be provided continuously to the functional divisions. Only in this way can the functional units update their personnel allocations across program activities and schedule in-unit work for those not committed to programs. This flow of information must be a closed-loop process, with feedback provided to the program, or matrix, managers so that they can make suitable adjustments where necessary to compensate for temporary manpower shortages.

The matrix organization is designed around the program activities as the principal organizational elements. The program manager is given responsibility and authority for his program just as in the conventional project management concept. In the matrix organization, the line or functional structure develops from the programs it serves, so that these functional activities play a supportive rather than a primary role.

The program manager receives from the supporting functional units a certain commitment of personnel needed to accomplish his program requirements. The program organization is thus composed of the manager and personnel on temporary assignment from various functional groups. Along with responsibility and accountability for successful program completion, the program manager has the authority for work design, assignment of functional group personnel, and establishment of procedural relationships. He may also have the authority to reward personnel with promotions, salary increases, or other forms of recognition while they are assigned to his program; and he has the authority to transfer personnel back to their functional group assignments as needed. On program completion, functional group personnel are returned to their departments for future reassignment, or in some cases are transferred to other departments to broaden their base of skills and their knowledge of the organization.

This process is not without its problems. First, it is rare that a program manager does in fact have authority to bestow salary increases and advancements on program personnel assigned to him. Frequently, many personnel are on part-time assignments to several programs/projects simultaneously. Authority to reward them must therefore reside with the employee's supervisor in his functional unit. Thus the fact that the program manager may be without authority to grant salary and promotional recognition and lacks other personnel authorities strips him of a valuable set of management tools.

Second, problems develop when a senior-level program manager has dedicated all his energies to a single program and technology for an extended period of time and now finds his program terminating. Unless another similar program opportunity arises, the program manager may have to be assigned to responsibilities involving a somewhat different technology—for which he may have to be retrained. This situation can cause hardship both to the employee and to his organization.

And third, the matrix structure complicates the client's need to identify a clear and immediate line of authority directly from the top (scalar principle). The sharing of authority between one program and several functional managers makes it difficult to pinpoint responsibility for actions taken, and can lead to sponsor frustration.

The matrix organization is designed to capitalize on the advantages of both the functional and the project structures. The coordination necessary for program completion is provided through the program manager and his team, while the technical support needed for high-technology development is provided through the functional area managers. The functional departments, although they exist to serve the technical programs, form the cornerstone of the matrix management system. These departments provide the ongoing base of professional authority and skills needed to provide leadership for the organization in its various disciplines. In addition, they supply a reservoir of talent needed by various technical projects and programs. In order to provide an adequate reservoir, the functional department heads should have access to discretional funds to conduct IR&D and to support professional staff temporarily during slack periods between program assignments.

Galbraith[11] considers the pure matrix organization as distinguishable from functional and project organizations by two features. First, the pure matrix form requires a *dual-authority* relationship somewhere in the organization. Second, there exists a *balance of power* between program and functional managers. Dual authority and balance of power are difficult to achieve and maintain in practice. Indeed, to a certain extent these two concepts contradict the basic precepts of good functional management. However, through enforced collaboration on budgets, salaries, and promotions, and in conjunction with dual information and reporting systems, this balance of power can be approached.

Nevertheless, such a dual structure inevitably breeds conflict within program and functional unit personnel. If the conflict is properly directed and is not allowed to escalate beyond reasonable standards consistent with productivity, this conflict can become a positive force and can motivate individuals to higher levels of achievement by bringing the program team together to resolve differences. Moreover, the matrix structure can, in principle, invite higher management to apply its broad perspective to joint decision-making processes, allowing the organization to achieve the high levels of technical sophistication and innovation necessary in our modern technology environment.

An Example of Matrix Management

Some organizations have successfully developed hybrid organizational structures based on a blend of project and matrix management archetypes. Battelle Memorial Institute* has experimented with such a hybrid structure in conducting both small, discipline-oriented projects and large, multidisciplinary programs all within a single organizational body. This has been done by structuring the organization so that its spectrum of technology is represented by a dozen somewhat autonomous functional departments, each responsible for a relatively well defined technological area. Routine projects of small to moderate size (generally, less than $100–$200 thousand) are assigned to the

---

* The organizational structure described here existed in 1976 both in the Battelle-Columbus Laboratories and at Battelle-Northwest.

single department wherein all or most of the technical work is to be performed. The project manager, who is permanently assigned to his technical department, can, as the need arises, borrow project support personnel and equipment from other departments, although the typical project is carried out substantially by the staff of his own department. This structure is common to many R&D organizations in managing relatively small programs.

To market and manage programs having large staffing requirements across several areas of technology, a special group of "senior program managers" was created by upper management. This group is not assigned to any of the technical departments, but has authority to cross department lines in drawing personnel commitments to meet special program requirements. The senior program managers are selected for their broad experience and ability in developing and managing large, complex, multidisciplinary research activities. They are given special title recognition and added compensation for their capabilities in this capacity. In the Battelle matrix management structure, the program manager has perhaps more of a marketing responsibility than a management one. He does not, for example, have payroll authority or authority to transfer people. Programs assigned to a member of this program management staff are handled much in the same way as projects under the matrix organizational concept.

While hybrid management systems of this type offer greater flexibility to a predominantly project-oriented organization, the dual-authority and communication problems mentioned earlier tend to be accentuated. Hence, the success of such hybrid systems depends on the ability of top management to regulate the dual-authority structure and intervene directly in serious conflicts.

REFERENCES

1. D. R. Hampton, C. E. Summer, and R. A. Webber, *Organizational Behavior and the Practice of Management,* Chapter 7. Glenview, Ill.: Scott, Foresman and Company, 1968.

2. H. Fayol, "Authority, Discipline, and Unity of Command," in *General and Industrial Management*. London: Sir Isaac Pitman & Sons, Ltd., 1949, pp. 21–26.
3. J. G. March, and H. A. Simon, *Organizations*. New York: John Wiley & Sons, 1958.
4. R. J. Cordiner, *New Frontiers for Professional Managers*. New York: McGraw-Hill Book Co., 1956.
5. J. L. Massie, *Essentials of Management*, 2d Ed. Englewood Cliffs, N.J.: Prentice-Hall, Inc., 1971.
6. G. A. Smith, "Program Management—Art or Science?" *Mechanical Engineering*, September 1974, pp. 18–22.
7. H. J. Thamhain and D. L. Wilemon, "Conflict Management in Project Life Cycles," *Sloan Management Review*, Spring 1975, pp. 31–50.
8. Robert R. Blake and Jane S. Mouton, *The Managerial Grid*. Houston: Gulf Publishing Co., 1964.
9. D. W. Karger and R. G. Murdick, *Managing Engineering and Research*. New York: Industrial Press, 1963, p. 299.
10. L. A. Bennigson, "New Approaches in Project Management," 20th Annual Joint Engineering Management Conference, Atlanta, Ga., October 1972.
11. Jay Galbraith, *Designing Complex Organizations*. Reading, Mass.: Addison-Wesley, 1973.

MANAGEMENT PRACTICE 3

Give the bird room to fly.

A number of conceptual models have traditionally been used to analyze and discuss behavioral aspects of management. The word "traditionally" may be somewhat inappropriate inasmuch as all such models have been developed since the mid-1950s. The growing importance of professional management since mid-century has motivated a considerable amount of thought toward finding simple ways of grappling with complex issues. Such models as those discussed here are inherently restricted in scope and applicability, and hence the ones considered to be more or less "proven"—as those here are—tend to complement each other.

EXAMPLES OF MANAGEMENT MODELS

Management models can generally be classified according to the different ways in which they focus on the employee:

—As himself, in his responses to his organizational environment.
—As a manager of a group of employees.
—As a member element of an employee group perceived as such by his management.

Other kinds of related models have also been developed, for example, communications models describing the mutual exchange of information in terms of authority roles. These, however, are not considered as management models and are not included in this discussion.

64

All the models described in this section are essentially non-quantitative. They cannot be exercised as predictors of future patterns based on past observations, except in the most qualitative manner. Rather, they serve as frameworks for thinking about and understanding complex issues. This can be extremely helpful to the manager who adopts models such as these as part of his technique for dealing with problems. Most of the models discussed here have not been developed with special reference to high-technology organizations and their employees, but reflect general behavioral patterns observed by industrial psychologists in the study of more conventional management and employee environments.

McGregor's Theory of X and Y Management

The prevailing attitude used by management in dealing with its employees is known to have a strong influence on the effectiveness with which the employees contribute to the objectives of the organization. It is clearly in the best interests of the organization to attempt to satisfy the needs of employees and to motivate them to greater achievement, if these objectives can be met without unacceptable sacrifice on the part of the enterprise.

During the twentieth century the industrial community has become acutely aware of the importance of employer-employee relationships and has sought to reexamine the roles that have prevailed historically. In order to effect useful reforms, it is necessary to have viable personnel management frameworks which can distinguish "good" from "bad" management practices. Such theories may then serve as standards against which certain other management practices can be compared. Since the field of human relations deals with the human being as the central element, it is unrealistic to expect a useful management theory to be essentially quantitative. Rather, a model of human management should postulate dominant employee attitudes about work and the organization, since management can then formulate specific guidelines on how best to harness these attitudes in the interests of both the employee and the organization.

It is against this setting that the theory of X and Y managements, associated with the writings of Douglas McGregor,[1] will be discussed. McGregor sought to explain management's policy toward its personnel by examining what management believes to be the general attitude of the "typical" employee toward his work. McGregor does this by constructing two polar theories held by management: Theory X and Theory Y. Each of these theories embraces a set of principles which, when taken together, can be considered to be the attitude of the employee as seen by his employer. The basic premises adopted by these two viewpoints are these:

Theory X—Basic Assumptions

X-1   The average human being has an inherent dislike of work and will avoid it if he can.

X-2   Because of this human characteristic of dislike of work, most people must be coerced, controlled, directed, or threatened with punishment to get them to put forth adequate effort toward the achievement of organizational objectives.

X-3   The average human being prefers to be directed, wishes to avoid responsibility, has little ambition, and wants security above all.

Theory Y—Basic Assumptions

Y-1   The expenditure of physical and mental effort in work is as natural as play or rest.

Y-2   External control and the threat of punishment are not the only means for bringing about effort toward organizational objectives. Man will exercise self-direction and self-control in the service of objectives to which he is committed.

Y-3   Commitment to objectives is a function of the rewards associated with their achievement.

Y-4   The average human being learns, under proper conditions, not only to accept but to seek responsibility.

Y-5   The capacity to exercise a relatively high degree of imagination, ingenuity, and creativity in the solution of organizational problems is widely distributed in the labor population.

Y-6   Under the conditions of modern industrial life, the intellectual potentialities of the average human being are only partially utilized.

If a management adopts one of these two philosophies it will tend accordingly to be either authoritarian (X) or permissive (Y) in its treatment of its employees. Thus, Theory X and Theory Y represent polar viewpoints, held by management, of the working attitudes of employees. By examining a particular management's personnel practices in terms of these two extremes, one can say something about probable internal employer-employee relationships and thus something about the human effectiveness of the business.

Theory X views the employee as lethargic and hence resistive to the legitimate objectives of the organization which requires his cooperation. Such a worker does not care to actuate his creativity; rather, he will carry out his assigned duties in a manner sufficient only to maintain job security. Since he is not a sentient being in his working role, pressure must be applied from above to make him constantly aware of his job responsibilities. Because he has little inherent desire for advancement, he is not motivated to perform his job effectively, and must be continuously controlled by his superiors lest he slip backward into a pattern of ineffectiveness.

Theory Y, on the other hand, considers the employee as self-motivated and committed to doing what he can to further the organization's objectives. He is creative and needs to express this side of his nature on the job. Management's control function is not to dominate or coerce him, but rather to offer him guidance and provide him with the job latitude he needs to express his creativity for the benefit of the company. His rewards go beyond the financial, and include self-esteem and peer recognition. In short, the employee likes his work and takes pride in doing it well. It would be incorrect, however, to interpret the Theory Y form of management as advocating the abdication of restraint, structure, goals, and objectives. This approach is not meant to indulge the employee. In many ways it imposes sterner responsibilities on him than Theory X does.

Historians of organizational practice generally agree that managements have moved closer toward the Theory Y philosophy over the decades. In bygone eras, most companies functioned under the proprietorship arrangement in which the head of the company was also the owner. He dictated personnel practices with a strong hand, since working conditions and the rewards for effective performance often were insufficient to engender satisfaction and pride in the employee. More recently, the corporate form of organization has separated ownership from management.

The size and complexity of the corporate functions have given rise to working teams, or task partnerships, wherein more reliance is given to individual effort. Another factor contributing to this shift from authoritarian to permissive management is that innovation often is a key ingredient for economic success in today's dynamic business climate. Rigidly controlled job descriptions stifle the employee's creativity, and his innovation potential is compromised.

This changing attitude is evident at all levels in the organization. It can be seen at the lower levels in the financial reward the production worker is given for his suggestion leading to cost reduction, and is reflected all the way up through the chain of command in seminars teaching creativity to top executives. Viewed in these terms, Theory X management is essentially static; and when it is practiced in today's competitive business climate it can be an easy rationalization for ineffective management. On the other hand, Theory Y management is dynamic in that it stresses the growth and development of the employee and challenges management to utilize human potential.

It should be clear that neither the Theory X nor the Theory Y management attitude is intrinsically "good" or "bad"; they merely represent polar philosophies. A concept basic to both Theory X and Theory Y is that of the "average" worker, an artificial yet useful supposition in dealing with group behavior; but a personnel management policy whose total emphasis is placed on the average man may have repercussions harmful to the organization when applied to the sizable group of employees all of whom are not "average."

For example, assumptions X-2 and X-3 profile the employee as needing authoritative control and direction to carry out his duties. It is widely recognized, however, that there exist *achievers* in every human population. In an organization these achievers may well be the most important resource, and their reaction against assumptions X-2 and X-3 would certainly limit or nullify their achievement in the long run. This is particularly true in companies which rely on creativity or innovation for their survival. Advertising, research, the theater, and education are examples of such fields. But even in what are nominally routine work assignments such practices can be increasingly oppressive, as workers become better educated, more affluent, and more mobile.

On the other hand, a Theory Y type of management is not well suited to the employee who does not have an attitude of commitment toward his work. The lazy or self-serving employee, whose values are not in tune with those of the organization, will require tighter management control over his assignments if he is to perform acceptably. If this attitude is typical of employees in a particular department, a shift in management attitude closer to Theory X may be indicated. Thus, while management attitude shapes employee behavior, the reverse also is true.

Maslow's Hierarchy of Needs

Social psychologist Abraham Maslow developed a framework that is frequently used in examining human motivation.[2] His model postulates a series of stages which characterize human needs, and stipulates that before embarking on the satisfaction of a higher level of need all lower stages must be satiated, or nearly so. Maslow's representation consists of the following five-level hierarchy of needs, moving from the lowest (primitive) to the highest (sophisticated):

1. Physiological
2. Safety
3. Love
4. Esteem
5. Self-actualization

The physiological needs are the most basic of all, and are common to all forms of animal life. When deprived of the means to gratify all the other levels of needs, man will focus exclusively on gratification of his physiological needs for hunger and thirst satisfaction. It is in the nature of man that, when extremely and dangerously hungry, he will set aside all moral and ethical values in his quest for hunger gratification.

If the basic physiological needs are relatively well gratified, a new set of needs emerges in man; Maslow classifies these broadly as safety needs. In contemporary society, healthy and well-adjusted adults are relatively secure from the forces of nature that once threatened primitive man. In a broad sense man now seeks the security of an orderly and familiar environment, where fairness, justice, and consistency prevail. Otherwise, the need for safety is seen as active only in emergencies, for example, war, disease, natural calamities, crime waves, social upheaval, or psychoneurosis.

The next level in the hierarchy is the need for love, affection, and a sense of belonging to a group. Suppression of these needs is commonplace in a modern world that is complex, competitive, and impersonal. However, if the love needs are removed or are lacking, the higher-level needs will be thwarted as man strives with greater intensity to reinstate or achieve these love needs.

As the physiological, safety, and love needs become relatively well satisfied there emerges the general human need for self-esteem, based on a sense of competency, of achievement, and of having the respect of others. The esteem needs are present in two forms. First, there is the desire for strength, adequacy, achievement, and confidence in confronting the world, and for independence of thought and action. Second, there is the need for prestige, or for having the respect and esteem of others. This aspect of need is variously referred to as recognition, attention, respect, importance, or appreciation. Fulfillment of the esteem needs leads to an attitude of self-confidence, self-worth, and competence, whereas when esteem needs are lacking one's feelings drift toward those of inferiority, incompetence, weakness, and helplessness.

The ultimate need, which emerges only when all lower needs have been nearly satisfied, is for *self-actualization*. This term is used to describe the inner motivation of a person to achieve and live up to his greatest potential. A person who lives in this stage of need attainment is characterized as one who is self-motivated to do his best at his chosen pursuits, without particular regard for the prospect of outside reward or recognition.

In discussing his needs hierarchy model, Maslow makes it plain that some people do not fit into this structured system as neatly as others. For various reasons, certain individuals project an inversion of these needs, or focus with unnatural intensity on one stage of need over other counterdeterminants. Also, it is important to recognize that the emergence of one need over lower needs is not abrupt, but can be perceived only in terms of degree. If the model were somehow to be quantified it would reveal that the average person's lowest needs are very nearly satisfied, whereas higher needs are satisfied in diminishing proportion.

Maslow's model offers several important insights into how managers should select and develop employees in high-technology environments. Presuming relative fulfillment of the physiological, safety, and love needs, the focus should be on enhancing self-esteem and developing the self-actualized employee. Esteem needs can be addressed by giving credit and recognition for superior performance, and by providing constructive advice and guidance when performance falls short of the individual's capability. Self-actualization is encouraged by liberating the employee as much as possible from tight restrictions and structure, and replacing them with autonomy consistent with overall job performance.

The Herzberg Motivation-Hygiene Theory

In his research on employee motivation, Frederick Herzberg published in 1959[3] and subsequently[4] a theory of motivation based on factors effecting job satisfaction. His original work was based on results drawn from interviews with some 200 engineers and accountants. An analysis of those results showed five factors standing out as strong determinants of job satisfaction: achievement, recognition for achievement, the work itself, responsibility, and advancement.

These factors, which Herzberg called *satisfiers*, or *motivators*, appeared most frequently among respondents who were describing satisfying employment situations. In analyzing job circumstances associated with dissatisfaction, however, an entirely different set of factors emerged. These factors, termed *dissatisfiers*, or *hygiene factors*,* were dominated by company policy and ad-

* Derived from the medical use of the word hygiene as meaning preventive and environmental.

ministration, supervision, salary, interpersonal relations, and working conditions. These two sets of factors, in decreasing level of importance, are:

SATISFIERS (Motivators)	DISSATISFIERS (Hygiene Factors)
Achievement	Company policy and administration
Recognition	Supervision (technical)
Work itself	Salary
Responsibility	Interpersonal relations (supervision)
Advancement	Working conditions

As a group, the satisfiers all describe the employee's relationship to what he does: job content, achievement on a task, recognition for task achievement, nature of the task, responsibility for a task, and professional advancement or growth in task capability. They are factors which, if reinforced, will lead the employee to higher levels of motivation, and hence productivity. The dissatisfiers, on the other hand, reflect the employee's relationship not to what he does but to the environment or context within which he does it. They involve the kind of administration and supervision received in doing the job, the nature of the interpersonal relationships and working conditions that surround the job, and salary.

The important distinction between satisfiers and hygiene factors is that the former are positive factors of motivation, whereas hygiene factors can only be made less negative—or at best neutralized—by improvements in the job environment. One can perhaps make dissatisfiers go away, but they cannot be transformed into satisfiers. To paraphrase Herzberg's analogy, if you wish to motivate an engineer by stimulating his creativity, you cannot love him into that creativity. Doing so may help to ameliorate his dissatisfaction with the way he is treated, but in the final analysis creativity will require that he be given a potentially creative task to do.

Since dissatisfiers cannot be transformed into satisfiers, it should be clear that organizational attention should focus on reinforcing satisfiers, not on neutralizing dissatisfiers. Improved environmental conditions and better trappings are nice; by themselves, however, they will not keep the valuable but disenchanted employee from leaving the organization.

Further examination of the factors reveals that among both satisfier and dissatisfier groups, increasing order of importance goes hand in hand with increasing generality. For example, an organization wishing to enhance employee motivation can address factors associated with responsibility and advancement much more directly than it can address those associated with achievement and recognition values. Thus, the more important a satisfier is, the more difficult it is to reinforce it.

The Katz Three-Skill Model

Robert Katz has presented an approach to managerial selection and development that has proved to be very popular since it was originally introduced in 1955.[5] This approach is based not on how good executives are in terms of innate traits and characteristics, but on what they accomplish and how they go about it. Katz identifies three basic and developable skills which obviate the need for identifying specific traits, and which form a useful basis for understanding the administrative process.

The first of these skills is called *technical skill*. This is identified with specialized knowledge and the ability to implement that knowledge in concrete situations. It implies a learned technology that involves tools and techniques, and it assumes that the manager has acknowledged proficiency in their use. Technical skill is both acquired through sound training and developed through practical, supervised experience. It is the most familiar of the three skills discussed by Katz because it is the most specific and most easily identifiable of them all.

The second skill is known as *human skill*—defined as the way a person perceives and recognizes his superiors, equals, and subordinates, and the way he interacts with them. The manager who has highly developed human skill is sensitive to and understands the behavior of and the role filled by his colleagues and his relationship to them. He projects an attitude of cooperation and responsiveness to his superiors, and works toward creating an atmosphere of approval and security in which his subordinates can express themselves without fear of censure, intimidation, reprisal, or ridicule. Human skill is perceived as being made up of leadership ability both within one's own organizational unit and in intergroup relations. As with its two companion skills, human skill can be developed through conscientious effort, namely, by perception, sensitivity, understanding, and communication.

The third skill in the Katz model is *conceptual skill*. This embodies the ability to see the organization as a total interrelated network of component functions, each dependent on the others. Managers who demonstrate high proficiency in conceptual skill are able to make a decision affecting one organizational component on the basis of that decision's ultimate effect on all other interdependent components, and hence on the organization as a whole. Katz suggests that conceptual skill indeed transcends organizational boundaries, and extends to visualizing the organization's role in the community and understanding the social, economic, and political forces at work in the nation or the world. Conceptual skills can be sharpened to some degree within the organization through apprenticeship with a supervisor or through special and rotating assignments. For the most part, however, conceptual skill appears to be an innate talent, and little can be done to develop it on the job.

Of the three skills, technical skill is the most important at lower levels of administration, although in the case of small companies this skill is equally essential at all levels. Here, the supervisor is working directly with subordinates whose efforts are almost entirely technical. To be an effective leader, he must have technical credibility.

In addition to technical skill, at lower and middle management levels the effective manager must also have human skill. Although important at all management levels, human skill is perhaps most needed where the number of direct interactions with different people (up, down, and laterally) is greatest. At lower and middle management levels the administrator should be particularly skilled in human affairs amid intragroup contacts, whereas at higher levels, intergroup skills are more commonly exercised. The need for human skill diminishes in relative importance at higher management echelons, where it yields to conceptual skill as the most essential.

Conceptual skill is, of course, vital for effective managers at all levels, but particularly at higher levels where decisions are made which must be based on integration of broad factors.

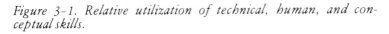

Figure 3-1. Relative utilization of technical, human, and conceptual skills.

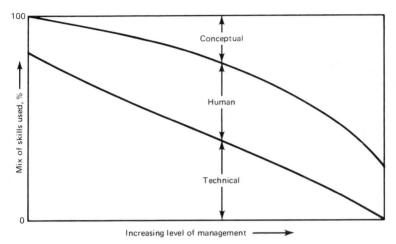

Figure 3-1 illustrates the relative utilization of technical, human, and conceptual skills at various supervisory levels in an organization. There is a direct tradeoff between technical and conceptual skills on the one hand, and management level on the other, as they are used in everyday operations, whereas the proportion of human skills needed remains more nearly constant. It is important to realize that the relationships depicted graphically in the figure concern skill *utilization,* not the extent to which the individual manager has developed and can exercise these skills. In high-technology organizations, particularly, higher levels of management must have strong technical capabilities in order to lead high-talent professionals, even though technical skills may be used infrequently.

Katz suggests that the three-skill approach is perhaps most useful in managerial selection and development. Skills, it is argued, are easier to identify than traits and are less likely to be misinterpreted. Administrative training should be aimed at developing those skills which are most needed at the level of responsibility for which the candidate is being considered. That is, executives should not be chosen on the basis of their apparent possession of certain behavioral characteristics, but on their actual possession of the requisite skills for the specific level of responsibility involved.

The Managerial Grid

The concept of the managerial grid was originally proposed by Blake and Mouton,[6] although the form in which it is described here is but one of the several variants that have been used to discuss it since it was first proposed. The grid is used to describe managerial effectiveness in terms of the manager's strength of commitment to the people reporting to him as measured against his concern for production accountability.

Figure 3-2 illustrates the managerial grid concept in terms of a two-dimensional representation of concern for the organization (production orientation) and concern for people (employee orientation). The effective manager demonstrates a balance of both attitudes, and the degree of his effectiveness is measured by the strength of his dual concerns. Thus, the manager who is located in area A is characterized as indifferent in meeting his responsibilities both to his company and to his employees. Time may have moved his performance back to this area from higher levels of commitment (the "burned out" manager), or his basic capacity for managerial leadership may always have been inadequate. Whatever the reason, this manager must be considered a poor one.

Likewise, the manager who is in either area B or C, while exhibiting a somewhat stronger level of concern in one direction or the other, lacks the overall strength and capacity for effective management. The manager in area D is viewed as relatively weak and as an ambivalent compromiser. He frequently moves from D back and forth between areas B and C (as indicated by the arrow in the figure) because he lacks the strength of commitment to balance his concern for the organization with his concern for his employees.

Managers of either the E or the F persuasion are considered by Blake and Mouton as equally ineffective because of their lack of balanced concern. These managers demonstrate an overall effectiveness on a par with that of the D manager. The G or the H manager comes close to the ideal because the strength of his

Figure 3-2. The managerial grid.

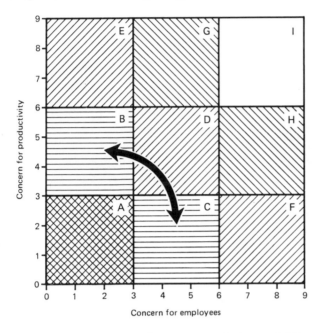

Adapted from Robert R. Blake and Jane S. Mouton, *The Managerial Grid*.
Houston: Gulf Publishing Co., 1964.

commitment to both the organization and his employees runs
high.

The ideal manager, according to the Blake-Mouton model, is
found consistently in the I area (the so-called 7-7, 8-8, or 9-9
manager). He demonstrates leadership in coordinating his employees toward fulfilling organization objectives and in developing their technical and professional skills to higher levels. This
manager also has a high concern for his own responsibility to the
organization, realizing that this is an important facet of both
leadership and personal growth.

The Life Cycle Theory

The life cycle model, as developed by Hersey and Blanchard,[7]
is one of the very few that draw from research in the management
environment of the high-technology arena. The model presents

an adaptive approach to management which can help R&D managers diagnose the demands of individual situations. It is based on the conception that professionals working in high-technological areas tend to be highly self-motivated and desire maximum latitude in conducting their work. The life cycle model postulates variations in effective styles of leadership according to the employee's level of maturity.

In describing the life cycle theory it is necessary first to define two related concepts known as *task behavior* and *relationships behavior*. Task behavior refers to the management mode wherein the supervisor exercises control over the activities of his personnel. It is characterized by the tendency to describe the role each member of the group is expected to assume and to establish well-defined patterns of organization, channels of communication, and ways of getting jobs done. Presented in its simplest terms, pure task behavior is autocratic dominance by the supervisor over his employees. Relationships behavior, on the other hand, refers to the mode wherein the manager relates to his employees on a more equal basis with emphasis on informality and social relations. It is typified by a manager who projects friendship, mutual trust and respect, and consideration for others' feelings. If task behavior is to be described as autocratic, then relationships behavior is to be considered as democratic, a contrast reminiscent of McGregor's X-Y dichotomy.

According to the life cycle theory, as the level of an employee's psychological maturity progressively increases, appropriate leader behavior not only requires decreasing structure and increasing consideration but entails reducing relationships support. Here, psychological maturity is used to describe self-motivation, competency, and the ability to assume responsibility. As an employee or working group progresses toward greater maturity, the relative mix of task and relationships behavior should change.

Figure 3-3 illustrates the essence of the life cycle theory. As an employee progresses from relative immaturity toward relative maturity, the manager's leadership style of behavior should change from 1 (high task/low relationships), through 2 (high task/high relationships), to 3 (low task/high relationships), and finally to 4 (low task/low relationships).

Figure 3-3. Life cycle of leader behavior in relation to chronology of employee maturity.

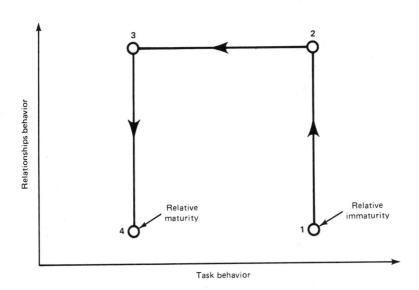

The R&D manager of a group which falls collectively in the 1-2 regime of Figure 3-3 must allocate a considerable amount of his time to direct supervision if he intends to enhance his staff's level of skill. Leadership here is synonymous with technical leadership, since the group or individual concerned has not yet achieved maturity to carry out work assignments effectively with minimum direction. In progressing from 1 to 2, the increasing maturity of relationships behavior is required to establish the informal communications needed to develop the employee's capacity for job-related creative thinking and coordination functions.

In contrast, the manager of a group identified with the 3-4 regime—that is, relatively mature employees—will spend a far greater portion of his time in planning, interdepartmental coordination, and acquiring funds and resources needed to keep his group productive. According to the life cycle theory, employees themselves become more self-reliant and independent in these respects as they progress from stage 3 to stage 4. Frequently, a group of employees will display a wide range of individual maturity. Effective styles of management must then vary from member to member in the group, in accordance with the principles described here.

Reddin's 3-D Theory

In studying factors related to managerial effectiveness, Reddin[8] was led to reject the notion of an ideal management style. Rather, he concluded that to be effective a manager must have flexibility to tailor his style to the demands of the particular situation. Managerial effectiveness must be measured as an output quantity, that is, what a manager is able to produce from a situation by managing it appropriately. Actual achievement is the basic determinant of effectiveness, but flexibility is essential to managerial effectiveness. The manager should be strong enough to maintain his chosen style under stress and not abdicate under a trying situation.

Reddin was careful to contrast managerial effectiveness with two quite different forms of effectiveness: apparent and personal. *Apparent effectiveness* is judged on the basis of appearance alone. For example, the manager who is always on time at work or at appointments, or who is prompt at decision making, may project an impression of effectiveness, whether or not the impression is an accurate behavioral indicator. *Personal effectiveness* refers to the extent to which a manager strives to achieve his own private objectives at the price of achieving those of the organization. This is a counterproductive form of effectiveness, characteristic, for example, of highly ambitious and self-serving employees, especially in an organization which has few clearly defined measureable goals.

In discussing managerial behavior earlier through the Hersey and Blanchard model it was proposed that such behavior is characterized by emphasis on tasks and on relationships. The degree to which each of these behavior patterns is present—according to both the Hersey-Blanchard and the Blake-Mouton models—determines managerial effectiveness. Reddin adopted this viewpoint as the basis for his 3-D theory. Figure 3-4 indicates the broad characteristics of a manager according to where he fits

Figure 3-4. Reddin's four basic managerial styles.

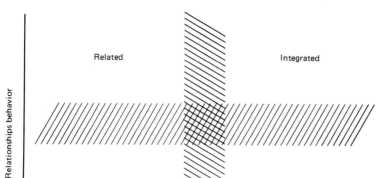

SOURCE: W.J. Reddin, *Managerial Effectiveness*. New York: McGraw-Hill, 1970. Used with permission.

in the imaginary task-relationships behavior plane. The four basic styles represented suggest eight different types of managerial behavior: these extreme styles are defined in Table 3-1.

To each of the four basic managerial styles shown in Figure 3-4, Reddin added a third element, *effectiveness*. Depending on the situation, one or another of the four styles may be preferred; thus, effectiveness constitutes an independent third dimension, and each of the four styles may be carried out in a "less" or "more" effective manner. The ultimate measure of effectiveness, as stated earlier, lies in the extent to which the manager achieves results. Figure 3-5 shows the resulting Reddin 3-D diagram, where each of the four basic styles may be carried toward lesser or greater effectiveness, depending on the abilities of the manager. The eight extremes of the four basic styles are defined in Table 3-1.

The essence of the 3-D theory is managerial effectiveness and its measure: results. In practice, this amounts to an adaptive management philosophy which adjusts differently to each and

Table 3-1. *Definition of terms in Reddin's 3-D theory.*

Lesser Effectiveness	Basic Managerial Style	Greater Effectiveness
Deserter A manager who is using a low Task Orientation and a low Relationships Orientation in a situation where such behavior is inappropriate and who is therefore less effective; perceived as uninvolved and passive or negative.	Separated	**Bureaucrat** A manager who is using a low Task Orientation and a low Relationships Orientation in a situation where such behavior is appropriate and who is therefore more effective; perceived as being primarily interested in rules and procedures for their own sake, as wanting to control the situation by their use, and as conscientious.
Missionary A manager who is using a high Relationships Orientation and a low Task Orientation in a situation where such behavior is inappropriate and who is therefore less effective; perceived as being primarily interested in harmony.	Related	**Developer** A manager who is using a low Task Orientation and a high Relationships Orientation in a situation where such behavior is appropriate and who is therefore more effective; perceived as having implicit trust in people and as being primarily concerned with developing them as individuals.
Autocrat A manager who is using a high Task Orientation and a low Relationships Orientation in a situation where such behavior is inappropriate and who is therefore less effective; perceived as having no confidence in others, as unpleasant, and as interested only in the immediate task.	Dedicated	**Benevolent autocrat** A manager who is using a high Task Orientation and a low Relationships Orientation in a situation where such behavior is appropriate and who is therefore more effective; perceived as knowing what he wants and how to get it without creating resentment.
Compromiser A manager who is using a high Task Orientation and a high Relationships Orientation in a situation that requires a high orientation to only one or neither and who is therefore less effective; perceived as being a poor decision maker, as one who allows various pressures in the situation to influence him too much, and as avoiding or minimizing immediate pressures and problems rather than maximizing long-term production.	Integrated	**Executive** A manager who is using a high Task Orientation and a high Relationships Orientation in a situation where such behavior is appropriate and who is therefore more effective; perceived as a good motivating force and manager who sets high standards, treats everyone somewhat differently, and prefers team management.

SOURCE: W. J. Reddin, *Managerial Effectiveness.* New York: McGraw-Hill, 1970. Used with permission.

Figure 3-5. Reddin's 3-D diagram.

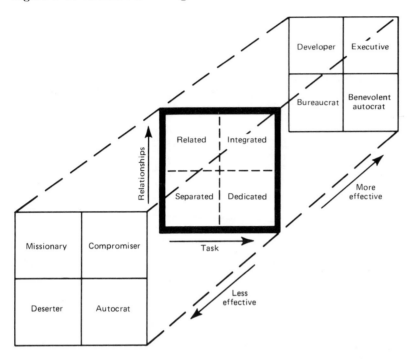

SOURCE: W.J. Reddin, *Managerial Effectiveness*. New York: McGraw-Hill, 1970. Used with permission.

every situation. Reddin suggests three attributes that are needed of any manager who is interested in enhancing his effectiveness through this form of adaptive management. First, he must have *style flexibility*, the skill to use a variety of styles at will to match a variety of situations. High style flexibility is exemplified by a manager who gets involved with people as individuals, not just as subordinates or co-workers. He does not see others as bounded by their role.

Second, the effective manager must have *situational sensitivity*, the ability to read a situation correctly. This characteristic refers to the ability to fit together scraps of incomplete and somewhat inaccurate information to develop the best possible understanding of a situation. Situational sensitivity can, to some extent, be improved with age and maturity.

Third, Reddin makes note of the need for *situational manage-ment skill,* which he describes as the ability to change a situation that needs changing through diagnosis, planning, and implementation. The essential components of this skill are the wisdom to balance human and technical needs and the conscientiousness to provide appropriate advance notice to the employees affected, thus assuring them of positive net benefits while avoiding any possible taint of a personal gain motive. These three attributes—style flexibility, situational sensitivity, and situational management skill—combine to make up what is usually called experience and good judgment.

Managerial Style: An Overview

Every manager has his own unique style, or way of doing things through people. To a certain extent one's style is a reflection of his personality and the pressures and responsibilities he must bear. On the other hand, a manager's style should be flexible enough to adapt both to the particular nature of the work being performed under his supervision and to the level of his employees' acquired skills. That is, an effective supervisor might choose to use different managerial styles in different management situations.

Most of the management models discussed earlier in this section focus on the individual employee: his needs, motivational factors, the managerial skills he should develop, and the nature of his relationships with his superiors and subordinates. McGregor's model differs in that it addresses the question of managerial style in relation to a group of employees.* Still, it is important to emphasize the relationship between management style and personnel, and the tasks they perform.

Figure 3-6 shows one way of relating the nature of the job being supervised to managerial style. Employees whose work is of a relatively routine nature requiring minimum skill and re-

* Certain of the other models, it may be argued, also address this question, such as the Herzberg and the managerial grid models. Nevertheless, managerial style in relation to a group is not their principal focus. Later on, Drucker's theory of *management by objectives* is introduced; this approach also deals with the question of managerial style.

Figure 3-6. Managerial style as related to job characteristics.

	EFFECTIVE MANAGERIAL STYLES	
Job characteristics	AUTOCRATIC	DEMOCRATIC
Routine	Structured, task oriented, centralized responsibility	
Creative		Unstructured, relationships oriented, responsibility decentralized

sponsibility usually respond best to a style that *tends* toward the autocratic, or toward McGregor's Theory X orientation. It is bad management practice to expect more in the way of responsibility and goal-oriented motivation than an employee is prepared to give. This does not mean that employees ought not to be provided with latitude to reach higher in these directions, but it does mean that expectations should match up with capabilities.

On the other hand, work that is of an essentially creative nature is performed best in a less-structured environment conducive to conceptualizing and to individual responsibility. Here, the manager's style should provide for more flexibility while at the same time providing positive leadership. This is the style suggested by McGregor's Theory Y management; it has generally been found appropriate for R&D organizations.

CHARACTERISTICS OF HIGH-TALENT PERSONNEL

The basic strength of any organization lies in its employees. This proven maxim is especially true in high-technology organizations, where professional engineers, scientists, and supporting staff must combine high-level skills and creativity in order to work at the forefront of technology. Employees of such organizations have emerged visibly since mid-century as a unique breed of people. As a group, they differ in several important respects from other groups of employees, and require somewhat different modes of management supervision. Stripped to its most essential quality, the relationship between the manager and the professionally talented employee in R&D is unique among all such relationships in that this employee is a highly skilled professional who usually is more competent in performing his particular job functions than his supervisor.

This characteristic is without precedent in management, and up to the present time surprisingly little motivational research has been directed toward examining the management of professionals in the R&D environment. Moreover, because of the manner in which managers in high-technology fields often accede to their positions, these people frequently are ill equipped to deal effectively with the day-to-day supervisory problems that arise. If the supervisory role were better understood in terms of the high-talent employee, both the organization and the employee would benefit greatly.

It is appropriate at this point to address a matter of definition. What, exactly, is meant by the term *high talent?* The focus of this discussion is on persons having unusually strong capabilities in scientific research and engineering activities by virtue of their training and experience. Within this context, the National Science Foundation has adopted a definition for *scientists* which may apply:

> . . . all persons engaged in scientific or engineering work at a level which requires a knowledge of engineering, physical sciences, or mathematical sciences equivalent to at least those acquired through a four-year professional college course.

This definition stresses the formal training characteristic of the high-talent professional, indeed an important component of his total professional profile. In the face of the rapidly changing, high-technology era in which we now live, it is improbable that a person can become a member of this group without long and serious academic study. The days of productive geniuses such as Thomas Edison (an American wizard of technology: 1847–1931) and Michael Faraday (the British chemist and physicist: 1791–1867), neither of whom had formal academic training, are gone. Even before their time Isaac Newton (1642–1727) said, "If I can see farther than other men it is because I stand on the shoulders of giants." Today, there are many more giants on whose shoulders to stand than in Newton's time.

Formal training by itself, however, is not sufficient to characterize a person as useful to the ranks of employed high-talent technical personnel. He must also have creative abilities and sufficient initiative to carry through his work assignment successfully. Hinrichs[9] has described high-talent personnel as:

> . . . individuals with a great deal of innate ability, valuable specialized knowledge and experience, and a high degree of personal motivation and drive to achieve their goals within the organizational framework.

This definition, set in broader terms than that of the National Science Foundation, stresses two essential requirements: (1) high capacity for productivity within the business (entrepreneural) context, and (2) high tendency to employ one's talents toward self-fulfillment. More simply stated, the high-talent employee must have high levels of both *creativity* and *motivation*, in addition to formal training. These two qualities are vital to the high-talent employee if he is to enjoy a satisfying and productive career. In view of the importance of creativity and motivation to the present study, it will be useful here to review their essential characteristics.

Creativity

Creativity is a subjective and multifaceted quality that has been studied quite extensively in recent years by social psychologists. Creativity cannot be measured by any single objective test currently available. Some creative people find it easy to work toward fixed deadlines, while others do not; the same is true of interacting well with others, having neat and orderly work habits, or any other such characteristics. Creativity can be judged only on the basis of past performance—beginning with childhood. The creativity present in an individual's performance generally is considered to be a product of both inherent abilities ("gifts") and environmental factors external to the individual.

The first of these concerns a person's ability to abstract concrete situations, transform knowledge from one area of application to another, and conceive unique and pragmatic solutions to problems. When these abilities are blended with inspired dedication, creativity becomes an inventive art. Creativity of this form is a valuable asset across the entire spectrum of technical endeavor. The pure mathematician who generalizes and rigorously proves a known theorem, the nuclear engineer who seeks ways of improving the performance of a nuclear reactor, the engineering designer who solves a difficult problem in instrument packaging— all these individuals must energize their inherent creativity in the successful conduct of their work.

It appears to be a fact of nature, however, that little can be done to infuse this kind of creativity in an individual. Some enhancement of one's creative abilities can be achieved by conscientiously striving to think in a broad, unencumbered way and to question the "obvious." Nevertheless, creativity by its very nature appears in substantial measure to be a latent part of the human psyche.

Environmental factors can be important to the venting or suppressing of one's creative abilities. In terms of the working engineer or scientist, one important requirement is the need for adequate equipment and other job-related facilities, such as a working environment conducive to uninterrupted thought, technical and clerical support, and the like. Without such equipment and supporting facilities it is very difficult for the creative individual to transform his ideas into working models or end results.

It is not enough, however, that the high-talent individual have adequate facilities at his disposal. One study of the factors influencing the publication output of over 3,000 academic, government, and industrial physiologists concluded, "If the conditions under which the scientist works do not allow him intrinsic job satisfaction, then providing him with the finest equipment and facilities may not stimulate him to produce. On the other hand, even the most motivated of scientists are not likely to accomplish much if they are hampered by a severe lack of facilities to work with."[10] This statement suggests that environmental factors are hygienic according to Herzberg's description, as discussed earlier. The organizational structure within which the project activity takes place, and the interpersonal relations which prevail, can also strongly influence the individual's manifest creativity.

It is of course of great interest to an organization to arrange its research activities in such a way as to capitalize on creative potential. Since little can be done to foster innate creativity among employees, attention must be concentrated on the individual's creative development within the context of the research and development team. This is an important theme which evidently has received little attention among management scholars who address the subject of creativity.

One of the earlier studies reporting on individual creativity among members of R&D teams in a number of industrial laboratories found, not surprisingly, that research performance rises to a peak in the mid-thirties, and declines thereafter.[11] Not so obvious, however, was the finding that chronological member age is *less important* than group average age, and that an older research person can often increase his creative output by being placed in a chronologically younger group. Thus, creativity requires both inherent and environmental factors, and it would appear that management has much to gain by accounting for the latter in its organizational structuring of research groups.

Management has a responsibility to itself to discover creative individuals and to maintain an environment conducive to creative work. Moreover, these efforts must be properly utilized so that the fruits of creative activity benefit the organization. The research manager can help foster an environment which encourages creativity; he can serve his staff by stimulating them, assisting them with routine details, and encouraging their creative activities.[12]

Special care should be taken in helping develop creativity in young high-talent professionals. Creativity can easily be stifled by placing such an individual under a domineering older man who may overcontrol his younger subordinate. The young professional should not be overloaded with work assignments, but should be given room to experience and develop his own creative processes.

Motivation

Creativity is also closely related to motivational factors which drive the high-talent technical employee toward achievement. Exactly what special motivational factors are important to this

class of employees? One might surely expect them to be different, at least in order of importance, from the factors motivating
other groups of employees in the labor force.

Hinrichs[9] has developed the following general hierarchy of
motivating goals on the basis of published studies in connection
with high-talent employees:

Highest:
    Personal success and achievement
    Intrinsically challenging work
    Company identifications

Middle:
    Work in a congenial atmosphere
    Upward influence in the organization
    Money
    Contribution to company objectives
    Technical orientation to the work

Lowest:
    Authority and power goals
    Maintenance of the status quo

Even from this general breakdown of motivators one can see
rather clearly how the goals of the high-talent individual may
differ from those of other groups. Among clerical employees, for
example, job security has been shown to be more important, and
job challenge less important, than is the case with high-talent
employees. This grouping of motivators by Hinrichs is again
similar in concept to that of Herzberg: the Highest and Lowest in
the Hinrichs model are comparable to the Satisfiers and Dissatisfiers in the Herzberg model. It then follows that management
efforts are best spent nurturing the Highest factors, since efforts
spent on improving the Lowest (which have to do essentially
with administrative factors) are less effective in the long run.

Many surveys have been made of the factors motivating the
high-talent employee's job performance. One interesting but neglected aspect of this question has to do with how the individual's values change with age and professional achievement.
Table 3-2 gives some insight into this question. This table was
synthesized from two separate survey reports summarized by
Hinrichs.[9] One survey (1955) was taken from a study of the career
goals of 626 outstanding graduates in engineering, business, and

Table 3-2.   Motivational factors as affected by professional development of high-talent personnel.

	RATINGS BY RANK		
FACTORS	GRADUATES	ENGINEERS	MANAGERS
Advancement opportunities	1	4	4
Challenging work	2	1	1
Enlightened personnel policies	3	8	8
Vocational training assistance	4	9	10
Facilities and working conditions	5	10	9
Company reputation	6	5	5
Community location	7	3	3
Salary	8	2	2
Company stability and growth record	9	6	6
Fringe benefits	10	7	7

SOURCE: J. R. Hinrichs, *High-Talent Personnel: Managing a Critical Resource.* New York: American Management Associations, 1966.

the physical sciences. The other (1963) was derived from a study of 1,000 engineers and engineering managers. The combined results can be presented in terms of the ten dominant motivators listed in the table.

If one accepts the progression from graduates to engineers to managers as indicative of professional maturity and achievement, some interesting conclusions can then be drawn. First, the rank order among the engineers and the managers was nearly identical, indicating that the high-talent individual has rather stable motivating goals once he has become settled in his profession. However, these goals change in their relative importance rather dramatically between the time the individual leaves college and the time he becomes involved in his profession.

This is due largely to the discontinuity he experiences in making the transition from the ideals of the campus to the realities of the establishment, but other factors such as new family responsibilities are also critical. For example, financial reward assumes a greater importance among engineers and managers than among graduates. Salary, however, tends not to be a strong motivator unless given as a reward for specific performance, where it then achieves a symbolic status as well. After all, salary increases must level off at some point, and at higher salary levels, because of the graduated income tax structure, the increase itself means progressively less in terms of purchasing power than it does in lower salary brackets. Thus, salary can be a sound motivator throughout the employee's career only if it is related to responsibility and performance.

The outstanding motivator—and the one perhaps which distinguishes the high-talent person from others—concerns the challenge of the work itself. The high-talent professional equates professional challenge with the opportunity for personal achievement and, in the terminology of Maslow, self-actualization. It appears that during his first five to eight professional years the high-talent employee concentrates on discovering his own abilities and limitations. Accordingly, he seeks positions in which he can learn and develop professionally, and places less emphasis on job security. Having come to grips with his abilities and limitations, say in his early thirties, he increases his organizational identities, and his need for security increases. This trend moderates as the employee enters his forties, when a new drive for professional achievement appears.

Equal in importance to recognizing the goals motivating the high-talent employee toward achievement is understanding some of the forces which detract from his performance. It has already been mentioned that challenging work rates high (if not paramount) among employees over a wide spectrum of age and professional achievement. Some of the factors which tend to instill work challenge have been discussed by Spitz[13] in a study published in 1970; these are listed in Table 3-3 in their order of importance to the respondents.

Adding to this list the motivational factors discussed earlier, it is possible to draw some general conclusions as to the attitudes of the high-talent professional. He wants to perform work that is both challenging and multidimensional—to stretch his abilities.

Table 3-3.   Factors contributing to work challenge.

FACTORS	PERCENT OF SURVEY GROUP LISTING FACTOR AS PRIMARY
Creative work	18
Broad area	17
Diverse assignments	16
Select own assignments	9
Work with things	7
Work with people	6.5
Group participation	6
Specialize	5.5
Work alone	5
Supervisory responsibility	5
Routine work	3
Other	2
	100

SOURCE: S. L. Spitz, "Satisfactions and Salaries," *Machine Design*, April 1970.

He is not strongly people-oriented, but willingly accepts interaction with others when necessary as a condition of his work. He has only casual interest in the organizational structure, and can be satisfied with any system provided it does not interfere with his job performance. Finally, he wants his compensation in direct salary and puts low priority on fringe benefits and other indirect salary augmentors.

Another aspect of motivational behavior that is important in understanding the high-talent individual is job pressure. It is widely recognized that employees—particularly professionals, executives, and other well-paid groups—are subjected to a variety of on-the-job pressures. Such pressures can accumulate and eventually result in degraded employee performance. It is not surprising that social psychologists and others have spent considerable time studying ways to relieve the pressure on employees.

But what would happen—in principle at least—if management were to remove all such pressures? Is this the often proposed ideal state toward which management should work to promote better performance among its high-talent employees? This argument has been challenged in a recent study[14] dealing with research scientists. Such individuals, it was contended, have a need to experience pressure to become motivated. Moreover, it was argued that this need is so basic to these persons that most of them will tend to create pressure situations artificially if such situations are reduced through environmental manipulation. Thus, pressures are not necessarily harmful; indeed, they appear even to be crucial to professional development. The low-pressure, relaxed laboratory—seen by many people as the ideal climate for research—may in fact be an ineffective, sterile environment in which to work.

This contention may be illustrated by considering the adjustment an individual must make in the transition from graduate school to first employment. Throughout his formal training years, the emerging scientist or engineer has a series of goals set for him: course work, other degree requirements, comprehensive examinations, the thesis or dissertation, and then its defense. These are fixed pressure situations which the student must face and overcome. After he leaves the university, however, few established short-range pressure situations will be set for him by others. The young high-talent employee may therefore set his own internal goal-directed pressures, such as achieving a certain publication standard or a job advancement within a certain period of time.

The Hall and Lawler study[14] involved gathering data on specific job pressures among high-talent employees. Their results showed the following distribution of pressures in terms of their frequency or pervasiveness:

Time	53%
Financial responsibility	28
Quality	19
	100%

They found that, while financial responsibility and technical quality pressures were useful both to the researcher and to his organization, time pressure was virtually unrelated to effectiveness and attitudinal measures. Time pressure involves both the meeting of deadlines and the continuous and effective use of time. This latter aspect was discussed in an earlier study,[15] which estimated the magnitude of negative factors (such as time spent on work beneath the level of the individual's training, duplication of effort, and inadequate facilities) that contribute to time ineffectiveness in research and development organizations. It was estimated that the average high-talent employee operates at only about 8 percent efficiency as a result of such factors.

Of course the R&D manager is ultimately concerned with the productivity of his professional staff. Productivity is certainly a broad concept and depends on many factors. In an effort to highlight the main characteristics of the productive R&D professional in practical terms, the Hughes Aircraft Company recently published the results of an extensive study on the subject conducted during the period 1973–1974.[16] The study included surveys of 27 industrial, government, and educational organizations, as well as consultants and existing literature on the subject. Table 3-4 summarizes the results of this study by profiling the typical productive R&D professional employee. The qualities described in the table all pertain to the individual and can be reinforced by positive, sensitive management.

Mention was made earlier of the particular need for fostering creative development in the young high-talent professional. Persons in their early or mid-twenties need time and opportunity to determine the extent of their creative abilities. In contrast, management problems do often arise with the older employee—problems having to do not with fostering creativity but with motivating. On reaching the age when they can see their careers coming to a terminal point (in terms of salary and position), many employees have a tendency to let down and coast into retirement. This attitude can be costly to the organization as well as to the self-esteem of the employee. The challenge lies in ascertaining how best to motivate the older employee who, in many cases, can significantly outperform those younger than himself.

While there are no clear answers to this challenge, incentives should be related to performance, to motivate older high achievers through promise of reward. These employees frequently associate job advancement, for example, with seniority, and have little incentive for continued high-level performance. Management should provide job challenges throughout the employee's career. Whereas job challenge is implicit in the work of the inex-

Table 3-4. Typical observations made by participants in a study of the characteristics of the productive professional employee.

On Employee's Qualifications

Job qualification is considered basic to R&D productivity. Without the proper job qualifications, high productivity is out of the question.

Is intelligent and learns quickly.
Is professionally/technically competent—keeps abreast of latest techniques.
Is creative and innovative—exhibits ingenuity.
Knows the job thoroughly.
Works "smart"—organizes work efficiently—uses time effectively—doesn't get bogged down.

Is cost-conscious.
Looks for improvement, but knows when to stop perfecting.
Is considered valuable by supervision.
Has a record of successful achievement.
Continuously develops self.

On Employee's Motivation

Motivation is a critical factor—a "turned on" employee is well on the road to high productivity.

Is self-motivated—takes initiative—is a self-starter and self-driver—has a strong sense of commitment.
Works effectively with little of no supervision.
Has a strong will to work—keeps busy.
Sees things to be done and takes action.
Likes challenge—likes to have abilities tested—enjoys solving problems.

Has a strong sense of urgency.
Is goal/achievement/results oriented.
Has a high energy level and directs that energy effectively.
Is self-renewing.
Gets satisfaction from a job well done.
Believes in a fair day's work for a fair day's pay.
Contributes beyond what is expected.

ON POSITIVE JOB ORIENTATION

A person's attitude toward work assignments greatly affects performance. A positive attitude is a major factor in employee productivity.

Enjoys the job—looks to it as the primary source of need satisfaction.
Becomes engrossed in the work.
Has good work habits.
Respects management and its objectives.

Has good rapport with management.
Takes direction well—readily accepts new assignments.
Is flexible—adaptive to change.
Is proud of the job.

ON MATURITY

Maturity is an important personal attribute. A mature employee displays consistent performance and requires minimal supervision.

Has high integrity—is genuine/honest/sincere.
Has a strong sense of commitment and responsibility.
Exhibits good judgment.
Knows personal strengths and weaknesses.
Is self-reliant and self-disciplined.
Is emotionally stable and secure.

Has self-respect.
Is persevering—productively works on an assignment until it is properly completed—gets the job done in spite of obstacles.
Is reliable and consistent.
Lives in the "real" world.
Has healthy ambition—wants to grow professionally.

ON INTERFACING

The ability to establish positive interpersonal relationships is a desirable asset that does much to enhance R&D productivity.

Is accepted by and interacts effectively with superiors and colleagues.
Works productively in team efforts—is cooperative—shares ideas—helps peers.

Communicates effectively—expresses thoughts well—is open to ideas—is a good listener.
Is personable—exhibits a positive attitude toward life—displays enthusiasm—is seldom moody.

SOURCE: Robert M. Ranftl, "R&D Productivity—A Key Issue," Astronautics & Aeronautics, June 1976.

perienced professional, it must be made available to the older
employee if he is to continue to improve his skill and feel that his
contribution is important to the overall effort.

MOTIVATION MANAGEMENT AND MBO

The preceding section presented an overview of high-talent
professional employees: who they are, their general behavioral
characteristics, and some aspects of motivation as related to the
group. In the present section a management framework will be
presented for mobilizing high-talent-personnel characteristics for
the mutual benefit of the employee and the organization.

The problem of designing and implementing such a framework
is an important one, since major management adjustments are
increasingly called for as our advanced "post-industrial"
technological society shifts into high gear. As organizations become larger and more impersonal, employees at all levels have a
greater need to fulfill their deep personal yearning for individual
participation. This need can be met only by decentralizing
decision-making authority, a trend which was begun in the 1960s.
Not only does such a goal benefit the employee seeking to become an important member of an organic body, but it also benefits the organization by upgrading the quality of decisions which
bear on complex technical issues.

Another challenge stems from our inexorable transition from
individual to team R&D. As in the past, the high-talent individual's principal allegiance remains with his peer professional
group outside the organization; however, to an even greater extent today than formerly, large multidisciplinary complexes
within a single organization are making it imperative that the
individual professional develop a spirit of partnership with his
colleagues, a partnership born of commonality not of discipline
but of organizational mission.

How management can instill this spirit in its professional employees remains a major concern. Both sides share in the responsibility. While higher management has an obligation to provide
an environment conducive to good work, the employee himself
has an obligation to direct his efforts toward organizational objec-

tives. The organization must not subordinate its interests to those of the R&D group. As has been said, R&D must be a part of the organization, not apart from it.

Still another challenge presents itself because of the conflict frequently found between the R&D scientist and the organization which employs him. The scientist often sees his main job as that of expanding the base of certified knowledge existing in the world, while his employer sees scientific contribution chiefly in terms of contribution to mission and/or to profit. These objectives are too often mutually exclusive. They can be reconciled only by concession on both sides. The scientist must learn to become more conscious of his entrepreneurial role, while the organization should structure itself to provide the scientist with abundant motivating opportunities.

Motivation Through Incentive

In examining the problem of employee motivation, it appears in general that motivation stems from two notions: (1) a perceived likelihood that a particular behavior is related to a desired outcome or reward, and (2) the value attached to that outcome. The importance of the value expected relative to the effort involved in developing a particular behavior varies from individual to individual. While one employee may be motivated to exemplify high performance because of the value he associates with the expected reward, another may be less inspired to put forth the needed effort because the reward he perceives is less important to him. Because of this, incentives—a major driving force behind performance—should be tailored to each individual to the extent possible.

Incentives are essential to the full development of high-talent employees. There are many kinds of incentives that management can offer as reward for desired performance. Incentives can be positive or negative, tangible or intangible. Positive incentives are those which relate reward directly to performance, while negative incentives are characterized by an inverse relationship and are therefore counterproductive. An example of a job environment exhibiting a negative incentive is one where more work is allocated to the more efficient employees, but without promise of proportionally greater reward. Incentives, to be effective, must be of a positive nature. The most visible of these are the tangible incentives, such as salary, awards and prizes, promotion, preferred assignments, and the like. Intangible incentives include recognition, approval, and group identification. The manager's task is to discover the particular mix of these incentives which is most effective in motivating a particular employee.

In striving to discover this formula—which may vary with each employee—two general principles should be recognized. First, the degree to which management can sell a benefit to the employee will largely determine its value. This is especially true in the case of intangible incentives, where value lies in the employee's pride in having achieved something few others have. If the employee is made aware by his management that a particular benefit is a symbol of prideful accomplishment, the benefit grows in value. Second, incentive rewards must, by definition, be scarce; the more commonplace they become, the more they lose value. Thus, incentives have a diminishing utility as motivators.

Promotional advancement is an effective motivator, although it does create problems with senior-level scientists and engineers who are near the highest technical level recognized by the organization. It is usually not difficult to identify the high-talent professional who is destined for management, as well as the one who is not. A problem exists, however, in discovering a suitable motivator or form of reward and recognition for the outstanding technical employee who has little interest or ability in a supervisory role. To cite a typical dilemma: Should the outstanding technical performer be handicapped by salary and title discrimination simply because he shows no ability in management skills, for which he was not hired in the first place?

One reasonably successful attempt to find a solution to this motivational problem lies in the so-called *dual advancement ladder* approach, currently in wide use. Experience with this process at the Westinghouse Research Laboratories has been discussed by Hallenberg.[17] Briefly stated, the dual advancement ladder approach recognizes as "separate but equal" the contributions to the organization by achievers of either management or technical orientations. Accordingly, a dual system of advancement is established for the high-talent employee who, at some point in his professional career, is destined for further advancement along either administrative or technical specialist lines. At each stage along these "dual ladders," management creates advancement rungs which are equivalent in terms of salary and title (recognition). Specific criteria are established for each of the rungs on each ladder. Thus, the technical specialist never faces the alternative of feigning administrative interest or otherwise remaining on some not-so-lofty branch of the organizational tree. He can strive for the technical achievement that will carry him all the way up to second-level management equivalency.

Hallenberg reports a high measure of success with this system at Westinghouse. He states, "The dual ladder system has gained wide acceptance among the professional personnel at the Westinghouse Research Laboratories . . . the holders of the [technical ladder] title of fellow, advisor, and consultant are accepted throughout the laboratories on a par with their counterparts in the management ladder. . . . Many professional employees, in the tradition of their academic counterparts, find fulfillment by individual technical contribution. Recognizing the importance of their individual work obviously motivates them and increases their job satisfaction."

The dual advancement ladder is not free from problems, however. The success of such a program is sensitive to the wisdom exercised by the individual managers who review and pass on candidates for advancement. If the criteria for advancement are not applied consistently among all functional units of the organization, the system may be weakened. Another important consideration is the organizational structure within which the dual advancement ladder system operates. If promotion along the technical ladder implies freedom from administrative or promotional responsibilities, then this environment must in fact be maintained if the system is to work. Also, many cases in which the dual ladder approach has failed may be attributed to a situation where a senior consultant has been assigned to a functional profit center, which misdirects his legitimate responsibilities. The manager, for example, may find it necessary to compromise the consultant's proper responsibilities in order that he contribute directly to program development or management activities which have a more favorable impact on his unit's operating revenues.

The dual advancement ladder method has also drawn criticism on economic grounds. As discussed earlier, most high-talent professionals choose to remain active in their technical work and do not seek management responsibilities. As a result, the supply of competent technical performers having strong management skills is well below the demand, and these performers are indeed a much scarcer resource than strong technical performers are. If one accepts the basic economic principle that the scarcest resource is the most highly valued, then the dual advancement ladder concept, which holds that both technical and managerial personnel are equally scarce and valuable, is not economically justifiable. If, however, the number of employees advancing along the technical branch of the dual ladder is small relative to the number of managers, then the method can be a good device for motivating the outstanding technical performer.

Combating Obsolescence

Because of the accelerated pace of technology, high-talent scientists and engineers are perhaps more vulnerable to obsolescence than any other professional group. Obsolescence as used in this context refers to the lack of up-to-date knowledge or skills necessary to maintain effective performance in either current or future work roles. Not all scientists and engineers, of course, become obsolescent; many combat this threat by taking positive steps to maintain currency in their areas of specialization. For those who do not, however, obsolescence may erode the value of their assets insidiously; it has been estimated that a scientist or engineer may have a half-life* of as short as a decade. Studies have shown that pure researchers are the least susceptible to professional obsolescence because they tend to stay at the forefront of a specialty. Production engineers, on the other hand, are the most vulnerable because they work in a broad area of applied

---

* A term used in nuclear physics to indicate the length of time required for a quantity of matter to lose half its potential to do work.

technology and find it more difficult to stay abreast of advances in related fields.

Combating professional obsolescence is a responsibility which lies primarily with the individual employee but must also have the encouragement and support of his organization. Continuing education programs are an effective combatant of obsolescence, and should be designed by both parties to integrate individual and organization goals to the greatest extent possible. Such programs can serve as a rich incentive for the employee to improve and update his skills, for both his own benefit and that of his employer. This is perhaps best accomplished through *training by objectives,* wherein the professional is allowed to establish his own development goals in concert with organizational objectives.

By far the most common approach taken here is through employee apprenticeship under a knowledgeable supervisor. Although this approach gives reasonably effective preparation (especially in the case of managerial development),* it is inefficient in terms of the time and effort invested. Another means is through organization-sponsored, in-house courses offered during normal working hours. Such courses can be designed to be short, goal-oriented, suited to answer particular organizational needs, and taught by in-house specialists. Still another approach is through correspondence courses, in which the individual employee can study what he deems most useful and advance at his own pace. This method is currently more popular in Europe than in the United States.

Wherever possible, organizational policy should provide the employee with time away from the job for self-learning during normal working hours. This makes it possible for him to pursue graduate-level training of a purely technical nature or in management or engineering administration. Provision should be made for assigning employees to such programs on either a part-time or a full-time (leave of absence) basis. In addition to expanding formal academic training, company-offered time can be used to increase training through professional society participation in

---

* Twedt[18] has recently compiled a list of references on management practice useful for self-study or continuing education.

seminars, committee work, and similar activities. There can be little doubt that these latter activities have been more effective in managerial training to date than formal academic training has.

In recent years several new multimedia technologies have been developed and are being effectively used in the field of continuing education for scientists and engineers. Among these are closed-circuit TV, audiotape cassette players, video cartridge units, and computerized learning systems. These techniques are attractive in that they are flexible and can be used creatively to suit individual needs. They suffer, however, from being expensive, and this drawback has thus far inhibited their wide acceptance.

The following elements are helpful—if not essential—for achieving the desired integration of continuing education with individual and organization goals:

—The employee's current and anticipated work requirements should be used to provide incentive for him to combat obsolescence through continuing education.

—The organization should periodically reassess the continuing education needs of its employees.

—One functional unit should be assigned the responsibility of disseminating continuing education information to all professional employees in the organization.

—Counseling should be made available to employees in matters of continuing education.

—The use of innovative techniques for self-learning should be explored.

—A feedback loop should be established for assessing continuing education programs, to determine which combinations of modes are most effective in fostering educational goals.

The topic of continuing education for managerial development is especially important and deserves additional emphasis. In planning their careers, the majority of high-talent professionals feel that ascension into management is the best and surest road to advancement. Unfortunately, many are motivated to follow this road even though their true interest lies elsewhere. Most professional employees agree that some formal management training is wise. Whether it is in fact wise is subject to debate, but this nation's heritage of exemplifying competency "by degrees" no doubt influences many to think this way.

Kaufman[19] has compiled some interesting statistics on the utility of formal academic training in helping high-talent professionals achieve managerial proficiency. Figure 3-7 gives the essence of his findings. Part (a) of the figure shows that in the majority of cases career expectations go hand in hand with the type of graduate program pursued. Part (b) of the figure suggests that engineers having graduate training in management ultimately find themselves in middle management more often than those who chose engineering graduate study, but among upper management ranks, type of academic training was relatively unimportant.* Kaufman summarizes his findings as follows:

> It is clear . . . that while engineers do need formal management courses to make up for deficiencies in their engineering education, the current evidence does not unequivocally support the belief that a master's degree in management is more valuable for an engineer's managerial career than a technical master's degree. The decision to pursue either degree should be based on a careful assessment of the individual's abilities, interests, and career goals.

Management by Objectives

In 1954, in his book *The Practice of Management*,[20] Peter F. Drucker proposed a broad management philosophy which, in the years since, has been applied at times within virtually every segment of our economy. More than merely a comtemporary buzz word, management by objectives (MBO) has become widely accepted as a comprehensive management approach which integrates all elements of an organization to permit management to pursue its legitimate goals for the benefit of all employees. It can be a dependable and flexible management process and serves as an excellent vehicle for training new managers and personnel. MBO has been tested within government, corporations and businesses, universities, and R&D laboratories. Its weaknesses in these environments have been identified and methods of coping with them proposed. Since MBO has proved its superiority over other contemporary management philosophies as an effective and specific blueprint for sound management of people (particu-

---

* With the increasing emphasis on technical management training, however, this situation may change as more technical people having management training find themselves in top management.

larly managers), it is appropriate to conclude this section with a description of the approach as applied in the high-technology R&D environment.

Figure 3-7. Career role expected and attained by engineers pursuing graduate studies in engineering and in management.

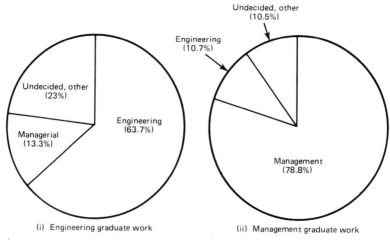

(i) Engineering graduate work   (ii) Management graduate work

(a) Expected career occupations for engineers who chose graduate study in (i) engineering and (ii) management

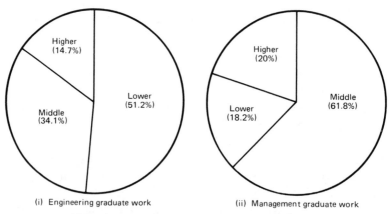

(i) Engineering graduate work   (ii) Management graduate work

(b) Management levels attained by engineers who received their Masters degree in (i) engineering and (ii) management

SOURCE: Adapted from H.G. Kaufman, "The Graduate Management Degree: Is It Really the Road to Success?" *New Engineer,* February 1974. Reproduced by permission.

MBO begins by recognizing that all forms of organization strive toward their own particular goals or objectives. In too many cases, however, these objectives are confused within functional units and among various levels of management, each of which often creates its self-serving interests. The result, then, tends toward unhealthy conflict and counterproductivity. An organization must synchronize efforts—line and staff, management and nonmanagement—so that each member will make his activities compatible with those of others for the common good. For example, within R&D organizations it is not uncommon to find that individual researchers—and indeed entire groups—are so consumed with research quality that the development of specialized knowledge becomes an end in itself. MBO emphasizes that their efforts must be redirected and coordinated so that they contribute in some specific way to organization goals, and that this can be achieved without sacrificing technical quality.

For effective job and team performance, organization objectives must be understood by all employees. To bring about this common understanding, each manager must first develop and set down in writing specific objectives for both himself and his functional unit. These objectives should embrace his performance expectations for his unit, what he and his team should contribute to other units, and what other units should contribute toward attainment of his own unit's objectives. These collective objectives should mesh directly with those of the organization as a whole as the manager perceives them. Moreover, they must be realistic and achievable, since unattainable objectives tend to have a demoralizing effect on the unit.

Under MBO, the unit manager must assume as his first responsibility the periodic establishment of realistic objectives in clear, unambiguous terms. This is obviously more easily done by some groups than by others because of their role in the organization. In the case of purely staff functions, for example, this can be a most difficult challenge, but unless a sincere effort is made, efforts may be misdirected. Hand in hand with setting his unit's objectives, the manager must establish appropriate standards for measuring progress toward meeting the objectives. In this vital part of the MBO process, measurements should be focused on the performance of the organization as a whole as well as on the individual employee's work. These standards should be established in such a way as to make self-control possible and discourage abuse by the control of people from outside or above, that is, domination.[21]

Once the objectives and standards of performance measurement have been set down, they are submitted to the next higher management level for review and approval, modification, or rejection. In case of rejection, the two management levels should coordinate closely to develop a modified set of mutually acceptable objectives. These objectives are then handed to all employees of the unit, and this is followed by a thorough dialog to air differences, clear up misconceptions, and bring expectations in line with capabilities.

In order to implement MBO fully, each manager not only must establish his unit's objectives with the approval of his own management but should participate in the development of objectives for his immediately higher management. This frequently has been done through the device of a *manager's letter*. At least once a year the manager writes out in detail the objectives of both his superior's job and his own (as he understands them), the applicable standards of review (as he perceives them), the things he himself must do to attain his goals, and the things his superior and the company do that help and hinder him. If his superior accepts this statement, it becomes the charter under which the manager operates. In this way an upward communication is established from manager to manager, which in turn forms the basis for sound cooperation.

The process just described appears to be a deceptively simple one. It presumes that each manager knows and understands the basic goals of the organization and how his job—and that of his unit—supports these goals. It also presumes that each manager is committed to making a "positive act of consent" to reach higher-level, achievable goals, and that performance is to be gauged by accomplishment. Finally, the process emphasizes the essential point that mutual understanding results not from downward communication but exclusively through communication upward. The superior will understand what he expects of his subordinates from direct "feedup," and his subordinates in turn will know what in the way of results they should hold themselves accountable for.

The MBO process as described above sets forth a set of actions to be taken by a manager. But what about the nonmanagement employee? In Drucker's concept of MBO the manager should provide an environment wherein each employee can function effectively as his own agent in contributing to his unit's specified objectives. First, the employee and the job are carefully matched. The employee's responsibilities must be in line with his training and experience level, so as to constitute a continuing and achievable challenge. The better this is done, the fewer problems will erupt later on. Second, high standards of performance should be established and enforced for the mutual good of the employee and his management. Third, the employee should be given the information needed to control his performance; this self-control element is essential for the implementation of MBO, for control from above or outside the unit strips the employee of initiative to perform to his fullest. And finally, the manager should give every one of his subordinates the opportunity for participation. This does not mean abdication of authority; rather it provides the opportunity for full expression by all so as to enable the manager to understand the needs of his unit and fulfill his stated objectives most effectively.

During the more than two decades since Drucker proposed the MBO process, it has been tested widely with general, although sometimes mixed, success. As a rule, where the method has been rejected as ineffective, that judgment has almost always stemmed from improper (or incomplete) implementation. Thus it is fair to say at the very least that MBO has yet to be shown to be either ineffective or unworkable as a management framework. Nevertheless, it is worthwhile to consider the history of experience with this process, in order to point out common pitfalls that have led to the "failure" of MBO. Most of these pitfalls can be attributed to one or more of the following common errors:

Overlooking Self-Control. The MBO philosophy advocates participative management. Frequently, management has failed to distinguish between the objectives that are stated and the self-control approach for managing managers and employees alike; in many cases the self-control element has been left out altogether.

Autocracy. Here, all objectives are wrongly established at the top, with the intention of extracting maximum productivity from managers. Realistic objectives, however, must initiate from the managers concerned, with guidance from the level above.

Stifled Participation. Managers must let employees participate in change and must help them develop new skills. The manager must be an agent of change and accept the responsibility of being a leader rather than merely an administrator.

Lip Service. Too often the manager endorses a subordinate's idea but fails to get involved in implementing it. Failure to guide or review objectives set by subordinates results in goals that are not congruent with organizational needs, with the result that the goals are easy targets which challenge no one.

Inadequate Feedback. The manager must see that reactions and positive suggestions on how to maintain and improve performance are continuously fed back to his staff.

Rigidity. Objectives should be revised periodically to accommodate changes in the economic, regulatory, and competitive environments, as well as shifts in authority and responsibility within the organization itself.

Inadequate Incentives. Compensation and promotion decisions must be directly related to improved performance and attainment of objectives, not on seniority or good intentions.

Expecting Instant Results. It takes time (often a year or two) and participation from all elements of the organization before results become visible. Often, either the entire organization has not been enthusiastically committed to MBO, or it has not been given sufficient time to make the system work because of fear of failure or misunderstanding of the approach.

As a process, management by objectives is well suited to high-technology R&D organizations. In particular, it is sympathetic to the human values characteristic of high-talent professionals in that it stresses participative management with individual responsibility and accountability. It promotes communication about and understanding of each member's role in the collective effort, yet places the burden of control on the individual himself. In these respects it is ideally suited to working organizations composed largely of highly motivated, independent-minded professionals.

MBO places a great deal of emphasis on planning and setting

objectives. It may then reasonably be asked how MBO can be applied to a highly project-oriented R&D organization where planning, to a large extent, yields to opportunism. Such an organization, after all, plays a statistical game of chance each time it submits a proposal for contract support. Although such an environment does indeed make close planning difficult, if not impossible, it in no way thwarts the setting of objectives. Successful R&D management relies on developing the right mix of personnel and facilities to capitalize on opportunities as they appear.

Thus the objectives set for the organization—and for each unit within it—to a large degree define the opportunities that will prove successful in the long run. Organizations engaged successfully in R&D contracting practice *directed opportunism*, which, together with appropriate objectives, makes the statistical game of chance considerably more deterministic. Program development is not accomplished by deliberate and consistent planning, but rather by intelligent awareness of potentials coupled with the seizure and exploitation of opportunities when they arise. The setting of objectives has a very clear role to play in providing proper foundations for capitalizing on directed opportunism.

TECHNICAL COMMUNICATION

Research and development activities rely heavily on the generation and diffusion of technical information throughout the R&D community. There are several different modes by which these generation and diffusion processes take place. Certain direct relationships appear to exist linking R&D productivity with how well technical information is communicated within an organization; it is therefore important that the R&D manager understand the principles behind these relationships. It is reasonable to assume that because of the close relationship between communication and an individual's technical performance, any improvement in the way he obtains, uses, and disseminates R&D information can have a direct bearing on the efficiency and success of his efforts.

Studies of how both management and nonmanagement scientists and engineers spend their time show that a considerable

portion is given to communication.[22] While there are many different ways in which communications channels operate within an
organization, they reduce basically to four distinct modes: reading, writing, speaking, and listening. Reading and writing, of
course, form a fundamental communications system, as do speaking and listening. Thus, all forms of communication can be considered within the reading/writing and speaking/listening systems. It has been estimated that across the population at large the
average person allocates his communicating time in the following way[23]:

Reading	4	15%
Writing	11	
Speaking	22	85%
Listening	63	
	100%	

These figures may be assumed to hold approximately for
both technical staff and managers within high-technology
organizations.*

Pelz and Andrews[24] have shown that certain relationships exist
between productivity and the frequency of communication with
peers inside and outside one's organization. To some extent the
sources and channels of information appear to vary with the nature of the R&D work being undertaken. This is especially true of
the reading/writing communications system, although the
speaking/listening system, because of the personal contact involved, uses sources and channels of information common to all
R&D activities.

The figures cited above show that a substantial portion of one's
time spent communicating is invested either in speaking or in
listening. Oddly enough, however, very little attention is given to
enhancing one's ability to speak effectively—much less so, to
listen effectively.

---

* Careful examination would probably reveal that, among high-talent
professionals engaged in R&D, time spent in reading would be somewhat higher, and in listening, somewhat lower. This would bring the
time allocated to the reading/writing and the speaking/listening systems
more nearly in balance.

Spoken Communication

Speaking as a communications medium occurs on two different levels: formal and informal. Formal speech signifies that the speaker "has the floor" in communicating his ideas before a group. Briefings, presentations, meetings, and conferences are occasions for formal speech, and skill should be developed in using them effectively. There are a few simple guidelines to follow in developing good formal speech habits; however, although these are useful, everyone must cultivate an individual style with which he is comfortable and in which he feels confident. Listed below are five basic principles which every speaker should adopt in developing effective formal speech habits.

Organization of talk. The presentation should be rehearsed to budget the alloted time properly. It should begin with a concise statement of the subject and the main thrust of the message, followed by the text, and concluding with a summary and reiteration of the most important points.

Foreknowledge of audience. The speaker should determine well ahead of time the expected technical background of his audience, the level of their knowledge of the subject or issue, and the degree of their interest (technical, political) in it.

Attitude toward audience. The speaker should communicate with the audience and never talk down to it.

Projection. Once an audience's attention is lost it is difficult to recapture. Effective speech embraces such style factors as eye contact, avoiding too much detail, and changes in voice inflection.

Anticipation of audience reaction. If a member or element of the audience is expected to have a hostile reaction to the presentation, regardless of its validity, the speaker should be prepared to do his best by persuasive rhetoric and responsive answers to questions to minimize hostile attitudes and gain acceptance.

Informal speech communication is the fountain of creative thinking in the technical world. The stimulus that comes from verbal exchanges with colleagues both inside and outside one's organization can be enormously effective in planting the seeds of new ideas. First, much benefit can be derived from explaining one's own technical ideas to others. This requires a sharp focus on basic principles and objectives, and enables one to fix or refine the ideas and understand them better. There is a certain psychotherapeutic value in gaining approval from a colleague who lends a sympathetic or encouraging ear and is considered knowledgeable in the general subject area. Second, the conflict of ideas encountered during the discussion can often be a strong stimulus to creative thinking. Such conflict can encourage inquiry, promote objectivity, and sharpen analysis. Thus, informal speech communication—often in an unplanned or accidental way—can catalyze a confrontation of ideas that results in innovative technical thinking. Some of the fruits it can bear are:

Information and technology useful in current R&D activities.
New materials, compounds, or analytical methods.
New product development and new R&D markets.
Stimulation of patent rights and licensing agreements.
Interest in or development of new areas of technology.

Listening

The ability of managers to listen attentively and conscientiously to spoken communication is a quality whose importance cannot be overemphasized. Without an attentive ear to hear their words, employees will not speak out as freely, and the flow of information upward through the organization is stifled—or, even worse, is cut off where it may already exist. Inattentive listening can also distort the purity of information flow both upward and downward throughout the organization. Thus, listening is an important quality for management to cultivate, especially in view of the fact that it commands so much of one's communication effort. Whereas normal speech is carried out at a rate of approximately 100–125 words per minute, one can listen at about three times this rate without loss of comprehension; thinking processes develop at an even higher rate—about 500 words per minute equivalent. Thus the effective listener is one who uses the difference between mental rate capacity and audio perception in the most effective way possible. Nichols and Stevens[25] have offered the following guidelines for enhancing one's listening capacity:

—Think ahead of the speaker, and anticipate what he is about to say. If you are right, you have reinforced your understanding of his point; if wrong, you can better understand his argument by comparing it with your own.

—Weigh the speaker's evidence supporting his points. The lapsed time between your thinking and his speech can be used to test the veracity of his points.

—Periodically review and summarize the speaker's points to fix them more permanently in your mind. This can be done whenever the speaker pauses as if to announce the beginning of a new point.

—Listen between the spoken lines for unspoken meanings the speaker, consciously or otherwise, may convey.

Recently the subject of *nonverbal communication* has come to be recognized as important to effective group interaction.[26] The speaking/listening communications system just discussed operates at both an intellectual and an emotional level. For the speaking/listening system to function effectively, messages communicated on an intellectual plane must be reinforced at the emotional level. Thus, to enhance verbal interaction, some facility in perception of the emotional—or nonverbal—communication level is essential. It can help in distinguishing what a person says from what he really means. The extent to which a person can be influential with others depends on how perceptive he is to the nonverbal communication both of himself and of his colleagues as individuals.

Posture is one important mode of nonverbal communication. Static tension (hands clasped, legs entwined about chair legs) and kinetic tension (fidgeting) can reveal negative attitudes such as hostility, anxiety, inferiority, uneasiness, or boredom. Facial expression is another important mode of communication for the perceptive observer. This applies especially to the amount and intensity of eye contact between speaker and listener. Relatively sharp eye focus is characteristic of a speaker communicating with a person whom he holds in higher status, or of a speaker who wishes to control another person or group.

Finally, speech characteristics can reveal the extent to which the speaker is anxious. As compared with the confident speaker, the insecure speaker tends to speak in complex, unfinished sentences, with poor pitch and volume control, and with nervous mannerisms. On receiving these clues, the attentive listener can attempt to interpret them in terms of the speaker's insecurities, and so determine what his own reaction or response should be.

All these forms of nonverbal communication—posture, facial expression, and speech characteristics—vary somewhat with nationality or environmental background as well as with psychological or emotional attitudes.

Written Communication

Written and published communication, too, is vital to technological progress. The way such information is used, and the extent to which it is used, depends in large part on the nature of the R&D work being undertaken (i.e., whether it is mission- or discipline-oriented). Pure scientists generally make greater use of published archival literature (printed technical papers that have been approved by anonymous referees) than applied scientists do. Engineers with a design or production orientation often make little or no use of "hard" scientific research literature, but rely much more heavily on handbooks, catalogs, and codes and standards. Thus the type of information used by the technical staff depends on where the given discipline lies within the spectrum—that is, from basic (scientific) to applied (engineering) information. Organizations having a highly applied or developmental orientation may be better off concentrating their information services in the form of reports, trade journals, and codes and placing less emphasis on seldom-used hard literature. Cooperative interlibrary loan agreements can be very useful in permitting organizations to invest resources in those published media having the highest technical payoff.

One of the most perplexing problems facing the scientific community today is how best to deal with the "literature explosion." Nearly every technical person is aware of this phenomenon: the annual rate of increase in world scientific literature (about 9 percent) is some three times that of world population. The causes for this explosion are many. Part of the problem lies in the fact that more persons today are finding their way into the scientific community. One device for fulfilling individual recognition needs is through publication—the creation of more technical information—and thus the problem feeds on itself. As a result of population growth and the increasing proportion of technologists within our society, it is estimated that approximately 90 percent of all scientists who have ever lived are alive at the present time. Since it is impossible to forecast an abatement of this statistic, one can expect a continuing increase in the scientific literature as long as scientists and engineers continue writing as they do.

But these reasons reveal only part of the problem and fail to do justice to either its magnitude or its complexity. The origin of today's problem of literature deluge may be traced back to the seventeenth century, when scientists in Britain and Western Europe recognized a need to coordinate their information exchange on a more formal basis. Up to that time scientific information was exchanged through the simple medium of personal letters, but as more and more people became involved in scientific investigation, a medium was needed to distribute scientific findings in a more effective way.

The French Academy of Science was the first group to act on this problem. In 1665 the Academy created the *Journal des Sçavans,* a periodical containing contributions from workers in various areas of the physical and natural sciences. From this humble beginning the number of technical journals has grown to the point where it has recently been estimated that more than 100,000 technical journals are being published at the present time. The number of these publications approximates an exponential growth phenomenon—with a rate which doubles about every 10 to 15 years.

Today's technical literature contains a number of different publication modes. There are, first, the technical journals composed of trade magazines, archival journals, and certain journals catering to statements of incomplete or tentative scientific findings, such as *Nature* and *Physics Letters.* Then of course there is a wide variety of reports originating from private industries, universities, and government laboratories. Most of these reports are not "editorially controlled," that is, they are without benefit of peer review by some anonymous authority. A few agencies, however, do exert some degree of control on their reports. NASA, for example, has an elaborate referee system carried out by its inhouse scientists. As a result of this system, editorially controlled reports tend to be more significant and polished than uncontrolled reports.

Aside from the technical papers and reports, many kinds of books are being published today. One finds, for example, tutorial "textbooks," handbooks for the practitioner, and scholarly monographs conveying recent scientific results in some particular field. Then, too, there are bound symposia proceedings, books of collected works by noted authorities, and anniversary volumes of contributions by various persons in honor of an eminent contemporary. Finally, there are a variety of "secondary literature sources"—indexing and abstracting services that attempt to distill and classify current published information by discipline or mission. These services range from title listings to authors' abstracts to critical abstracts prepared by competent scientific authorities.

How can the R&D manager effectively cope with this overpowering glut of printed technical information? First, it must be realized that scientists and technologists have rather firmly established patterns for information exchange; these must be understood before any attempt is made to modify or improve information services.[27] Some of these have already been discussed. Then, too, recent decades have witnessed changes in the social organization of R&D which have led away from individual inquiry toward collaborative team research. With each passing decade the technical literature contains more and more multi-authored reports and articles—in striking contrast to the almost unchanging character of single-authored papers in the humanities.[28] Moreover, in their quest to obtain recognition and priority of R&D findings through rapid and frequent publication, members of the technical community are under pressure to publish work that is tentative, speculative, or otherwise incomplete, even to the point that the scientist or engineer will often resort to fragmentation, that is, splitting a complete R&D study into several overlapping units for multiple publication in one or more journals.

In the foreseeable future technology will strive to manage the information deluge by several means:

—A growing tendency away from traditional journal formats toward greater use of preprints distributed by the author and announced through abstracting and indexing services.

—Increases in the number of abstracting and indexing services, with more emphasis on timeliness and less on criticality of abstracts.

—Involvement of technical and scientific societies that will set higher standards and sanction groups of journals on the basis of quality and timeliness. Submission and acceptance/rejection information would be shared by all members of each group.

—Advances in typography that will permit more rapid (although perhaps less elegant) typesetting of articles for printed publication.

—More rigid standards for titles and abstracts, coupled with more extensive use of electronic data processing, to facilitate improved information retrieval.

There are a number of more or less controllable factors which influence the degree to which information is used by and diffused through an organization. The value an organization places on such use and dissemination distinctly influences the information behavior within it. Here, the term *value* is subjectively measured by the willingness of the organization to support professional involvement and participation in technical meetings designed to enhance its R&D creativity. The physical grouping of persons also influences the degree of communications interaction. The sociological concept of "residential propinquity" applies here: studies have shown that spontaneous interactions among persons fall off sharply when desks or offices are separated by more than a few steps.

Individuals themselves differ strongly in the degree to which they absorb and transmit new information. The term *high communicator* has been applied to describe those rare individuals whose ability to absorb and communicate information greatly exceeds the average.[22] These persons are considered by their peers as both gatekeepers and distributors of information, and their counsel is frequently sought. They are usually among the most productive employees, and technical managers have much to gain by working toward identifying, developing, and strategically placing these individuals within the organization.

Communications Management

Having described some of the characteristics of communications systems within R&D organizations, the question arises as to what all this means to the manager. What exactly is the manager's role in fostering good communications and the free flow of information within his organization?

First, the manager should ensure that a thorough working communications system functions within his unit. It is important not only that he establish appropriate mechanisms but also that he project a positive attitude concerning the importance of communications and so set the right kind of example for other employees. Regular staff meetings should be held to exchange management information, to discuss operations and planning, and to solve problems. Meetings should be brief, and where agenda are appropriate, they should be distributed in advance to all participants so that they will be properly prepared beforehand. Where possible, meetings should involve participants of more or less equal status, and the chairman should see to it that a specific set of conclusions and/or action items emerges from the meeting, with responsibilities for follow-up clearly understood by all concerned. In addition to meetings and briefings, the manager should ensure that all memoranda and reports of relevant interest to his staff are circulated. This serves not only to diffuse information through the department but also to inspire an attitude of individual importance and participation on the part of the technical staff.

Second, management should strive to identify and develop those among the staff who have the potential to be high communicators. This can be achieved only if the manager stays close to the actual technical process for which he is responsible. Employees having the characteristics of the high communicator should be placed, both physically and organizationally, where they can interact most effectively with others of similar technical background.

Finally, the manager must be cognizant of his need to develop good communications skills among his staff. This can be done by providing the opportunities for participation in in-house technical meetings and seminars as well as in professional meetings and committee work. Summaries of these activities should be distributed to those who can best make use of the information. The manager can also help develop communications skills through example by providing a free flow of information. Part of the manager's responsibility, after all, is to develop his staff, and a fruitful apprenticeship requires a good teacher.

APPROACHES TO STAFFING

The continued growth and strength of an organization is only as sound as its ability to maintain a proficient staff. Most high-technology organizations focus their staffing efforts at the technical levels, since a strong technical/professional staff is essential for R&D operations. Such a focus is indeed proper. However, the managers of an organization must also anticipate future needs for management personnel, to ensure an adequate pool of both technical staff and management candidates. The importance—and problems—of planning for the desired future blend of technical and managerial personnel is the subject of a monograph by Vetter.[29] There he brings out the fact that the lead times required for recruiting, training, and developing high-talent professionals is much longer than for other employee groups, therefore compounding manpower planning problems.

Examination of available statistics indicates that under conditions of economic growth the future supply of those qualified for professional, technical, and managerial positions will, at best, barely satisfy the demand. Moreover, finding qualified management talent at all levels is becoming increasingly important in R&D organizations. One indication of this trend lies in the fact that immediately following World War II, less than 10 percent of U.S. management was trained in the sciences and engineering; today the figure is approximately 25 percent. Because of the rapid acceleration of technology, it becomes more difficult to count on internal adaptation to supply professional and management needs; the right person must be at the right place at the right time. This can be ensured only through planning.

Manpower Planning

Manpower planning is the process by which management determines how the organization should move from its current manpower position to its desired or projected position. Although well established in most large private and commercial organizations, this function is relatively new to R&D organizations. Manpower planning has as its objectives to enrich opportunities for individual growth and development and to help the organization meet current manpower needs and anticipate those of the future. Through planning, management strives to have the right number and kinds of people, at the right places at the right times, doing things that will result in maximum long-run benefit for both the organization and the individual.

Formal manpower planning is most useful with relatively large organizations and with those that are centralized. In such organizations the personnel department, under which manpower planning functions normally fall, usually holds the authority needed to create and implement such programs for the functional departments. The manpower planning program would then consist in integrating management development, manpower forecasting, and organizational planning activities. In the smaller or highly decentralized R&D structure, organized manpower planning tends to be much less effective.

Many of the larger high-technology organizations have introduced management development programs to ensure a continued diffusion of talent upward from the technical to the management ranks. While such programs are good in themselves, they may be inadequate to meet future management needs. After all, merely having a sufficient pool of management candidates is insufficient if those candidates are not well suited to future requirements. Moreover, a low management turnover rate may be a poor index of current managerial effectiveness; it may indicate an abundance of managers whom no one else would want. The success of a manpower planning program can best be measured by whether the organization has the management personnel it requires when needed. In order to bring this about, the planner must have access to higher management's blueprint of future organizational directions and needs.

Organizations vary in their philosophy on how best to plan for future professional and management needs. Some approach the recruiting phase by hiring only high achievers, strong individuals who show immediate promise of developing into the kinds of talent that are consistent with planned needs. Despite the obvious merits of this approach, there are drawbacks, most especially in lowered morale of present employees whose chances for advancement appear thwarted. Many organizations choose to hire a number of average performers along with selected high achievers. This is done on the presumption that under proper leadership some proportion of the former will develop into strong managers, while the rest will serve continually to infuse the technical ranks with new capabilities and ideas.

Vetter[29] has provided a list of manpower planning functions to help in evaluating the current status of such programs within an organization. It is presented in somewhat modified form in Figure 3-8. It serves as a useful checklist to help identify areas where manpower management is weak and planning is required.

Interviewing

Having discussed a general approach to managerial manpower staffing, it is appropriate now to turn to the specific mechanics of the employment interview process. Manpower planning is used to set goals for ensuring adequate staffing commensurate with projected needs. Employment interviewing, on the other hand, embraces a set of procedures for implementing the planning activity.

As usually practiced, employment interviewing consists of ten successive steps, although which of these steps actually apply depends on the position being filled, the size and nature of the organization, and the particular situation of the applicant. Large organizations usually have rather structured hiring practices for all but the higher management echelons. In such cases the following chronology of steps is customarily found:

1. *Job description.* Here the specific responsibilities and degree of authority are laid out in detail for the position to be filled. This step serves to define the characteristics and experience level of the employee being sought.

2. *Recruiting.* In this step, in conjunction with the operating department concerned, the personnel department attempts to define the sources for likely candidates and the probable talent

Figure 3-8. Functions of the manpower management program.

PLANNING

Maintaining an adequate information system on management manpower.

Anticipating future managerial manpower requirements.

Providing sound promotion and career opportunities for managers.

Identifying objectives for management development programs.

Identifying career mobility patterns for managers.

Anticipating organizational design changes and preparing for manpower implications.

Researching the causes and solutions of serious manpower problems.

Establishing meaningful objectives of manpower management programs.

Integrating the manpower management program with organizational objectives to achieve greater overall success.

IMPLEMENTING

Recruiting the desired number of qualified people from college.

Effectively placing newly hired young managers to make them productive.

Adequately evaluating the current performance of managers.

Adequately evaluating the potential of managers for higher responsibilities.

Filling key middle and top management positions with qualified persons.

Reducing attrition among capable managers at all levels.

Keeping the management compensation system up to date and effective as a motivator.

Developing managers for higher-level responsibilities.

Helping experienced managers to fight obsolescence.

Motivating managers to develop subordinates effectively.

Providing meaningful job assignments for managers throughout their careers.

Managing the retirement pattern to help prevent replacement problems.

Obtaining top management and organizational support for manpower management programs.

Measuring the labor productivity improvements of the workforce.

SOURCE: Adapted from Eric W. Vetter, *Manpower Planning for High Talent Personnel*. Ann Arbor: University of Michigan Press, 1967.

locators. The objective is to pinpoint a sufficiently large pool of candidates so that the initial screening (step 3) is sure to result in several prospects well suited to the job requirements.

3. *Initial screening.* The candidates suggested from the recruiting phase (step 2) are sorted out on the basis of available information (perhaps a preapplication) to retain all but the obviously unfit for further consideration.

4. *Application blank.* The form of the written application is a vital piece of information. It should be designed to the level of qualifications being sought (e.g., clerical, subprofessional, professional, and management). All relevant factual data should be called for to help make possible a thorough and objective final evaluation.

5. *Personal interview.* This step is the heart of the employment interview process, and will be discussed in some detail below.

6. *Reference check.* At least three persons in a position to respond in detail and objectively should be contacted by telephone (aside from being slow, letters produce much less information than an informal conversation does). Several points should be probed; for example, when and where the applicant worked (including a verification of dates), salary history, work quality, and attendance and accident record. A candid reply to the question "Would you rehire the applicant today?" can be most revealing. Often the reference check precedes the personal interview and is used as a screening tool.

7. *Testing.* Many organizations use psychological and/or vocational testing to determine skills and work potential levels. Although federal restrictions have recently curbed major areas of psychological testing, much can be learned through nonstandardized tests designed to probe the mental, emotional, and manual skills required for the job. This step is used to determine the degree of "can do" as opposed to the "will do" established in steps 5 and 6.

8. *Physical examination.* The applicant should undergo a thorough physical examination, on his own or through organizational resources for mutual protection in the event of hire.

9. *Final screening.* At this stage, all paperwork for each appli-

cant is carefully evaluated and compared with the others, to determine which of the applicants will receive an offer of employment.

10. *Hiring.* The successful applicant is extended an offer of employment. In the case of higher-level professional or management positions, salary, benefits, and other conditions of employment may be subject to some negotiation. When all details are agreed upon an employment contract is signed by both parties.

Step 5, the personal interview, lies at the heart of the employment interview process and yet is surprisingly often the most neglected step. There is an art to effective interviewing, but like any art it can be sharpened through greater understanding and appreciation of basic principles. A personal interview session is usually conducted over a short interval of time, often as little as one hour. The most effective possible use must be made of this time, for the information being sought will be influential in a most important decision: whether or not to hire.

The most common errors committed by the interviewer during the interview all stem from ineffective use of this valuable time. For example, one common error is to spend the entire time dwelling on amenities and chatting about familiar people, places, or areas of interest that have nothing to do with the central issues. While this does avoid the burden of effort and confrontation of ideas, it represents an unfortunate waste of a valuable opportunity. Other errors committed by the interviewer are to do most of the talking and little listening, and to neglect to probe more deeply behind first-level responses to questions.

A well-structured personal interview generally proceeds as follows. First a few minutes are spent in small talk to establish rapport. Then the interviewer directs the interview into what may be called the contract stage. At this point the applicant is told why he is there, and is informed that he must be asked certain questions to enable a fair evaluation. This brief introduction serves to place both parties on a common basis of understanding.

Following this the interviewer begins to question the applicant, initially about broad issues, then narrowing down to specifics. The applicant should be controlled by the interviewer, and not allowed to give a rehearsed presentation. What was the nature of the applicant's most recent position, his salary, the number of persons he supervised, and his reason for leaving? These same questions are then addressed to the next most recent job, and so on. What about military experience, appointments, volunteer activities, and part-time jobs? What were the most and least satisfying positions, and who were the most and least favored supervisors?

The interviewer should bore into apparent contradictions and not overlook them out of false courtesy. Questions may then lead to factors such as health, education, family, and use of free time. During this process the interviewer should continually direct the questions toward narrower and more personal issues. Attitudes toward brothers and sisters can be revealing, since they parallel the applicant's likely attitude toward others of similar personality. He may also be asked to comment on his attitudes concerning his parents, wife or husband, friends, drinking and gambling habits, hobbies, politics, and favorite books and TV programs. Finally—and importantly—the applicant should project himself into the future by explaining what he wishes to be doing, say, five years hence.

During this entire process the applicant has been doing almost all the talking within the guidelines set by the interviewer's questions. When all the desired information has been gathered, the applicant is briefed on the job requirements and working environment. Here he should be encouraged to ask questions related to the position being sought, for such questions can provide insight into his grasp of the job. Following the formal interview, a person in authority should tell the applicant when, specifically, he can expect to hear about the status of his application.

The procedure just described addresses the problem of locating and interviewing prospective employee candidates. The circumstances assumed require that the candidate being interviewed attempt to sell himself to the organization, and that the interviewer's role be to decide whether or not to extend an offer. There are times, however, when these roles are reversed and the organization must try to sell itself to the interviewee. This may happen if the balance between supply and demand tips heavily in favor of the job seeker, or, more commonly, when an organization attempts to hire a person whose reputation makes it known beforehand that he will be a prized addition to the technical staff. Under these circumstances the organization's management and technical personnel are challenged to win the candidate by emphasizing the job opportunities being offered.

PROFESSIONAL DEVELOPMENT

Individuals working at professional levels in high-technology occupations have an obligation to themselves and society to contribute a part of their skills and talents to further the goals of organized technology. Professionalism is too broad a concept to define satisfactorily. It involves that part of one's total contribution to technology which goes beyond the day-to-day, task-oriented responsibilities. Indeed, one of the characteristics which sets the professional apart from other technically oriented individuals is his ability to pursue broad goals with little direct supervision. Such a person is in effect an integrator who coordinates the various technical tasks needed to accomplish technical objectives. Whether he does this alone or as a member of a team is immaterial; it is his goal-oriented attitude which qualifies him as a professional.

There are other trademarks of a professional, however, and these are equally important. The professional person is a member of a specialized technical "community," which is generally regarded by society at large as the foremost repository of knowledge in its field. Each member of this technical community must be an active contributor so that the repository can continue to meet the needs of the society in which it functions. The professional's responsibility to society obligates him to be not only a consumer of knowledge but a developer and a dispenser as well. Another trademark of the professional is that he manifests a high degree of independence of action in carrying out his short- and long-range activities. This quality derives from the essential characteristic of the professional: he is goal-, not task-oriented.

It is important both to himself and to his organization that the employee become an active and vital part of his technical profession. One important reason for this is that the professional employee's potential for peer recognition is much greater among colleagues outside his organization than among those within it. Thus "professionalism," in the sense used here, can serve to reinforce the esteem needs described by Maslow and can encourage the employee toward realization of his capacity for self-actualization. Any strengthening of these higher levels of human need can only enhance the employee's value to himself and to his organization.

There are other important reasons for management to encourage professionalism among its technical staff. One is that through informal exchanges with colleagues in other organizations and institutions the employee is in a far better position to sharpen his technical skills than if he remains in his isolated environment at home. The more varied the inputs and ideas he can assimilate from others, the more creative—innovative—he can become. Moreover, through participation in professional activities he gains valuable experience in planning and leadership roles. Involvement in such activities also creates a greater awareness of the interdependencies among related technical disciplines. This kind of perspective is essential if professionals are to become truly goal-oriented.

Innumerable opportunities for engaging in professional activities are available. Indeed, one of the problems facing the conscientious professional is how to choose those activities that will be best both for him and for his organization, and that he can pursue without undue compromise of his day-to-day responsibilities. A wide variety of technical societies, both national and international in scope, are constantly in need of talented professionals willing to volunteer their time. Technical personnel have responsibilities not only for publishing the results of their own work when appropriate but also for fostering publication by others in their field through reviewing activities on behalf of journals and similar media.

Further opportunities for professional involvements are available through direct participation in symposia and technical meetings, both in the organizing phases and by delivering technical presentations. More recently, professionals engaged in high-technology endeavors have awakened to their opportunities in the political arena. Society at large in developed nations is heavily dependent on advances in technology; legislators and policy makers—and hence society—can benefit greatly from the counsel of informed members of the technical community.

In addition to professional involvements of the nature just described, employees have a responsibility for fostering their own professional development in other ways. Most importantly, they must maintain their technical competence. As discussed earlier in this chapter under the heading "combating obsolescence," continuing education, both formal and self-administered, is essential to technical viability. Professional registration or certification, where appropriate, should be achieved as soon as possible.

While all technology-based organizations have a self-interest in fostering professional involvement on the part of their employees, there are limits to such involvements. It is possible for an employee to become a *professional professional* whose usefulness to his organization is compromised by excessive outside commitments. However, it is unusual for an organization to have to restrict its employees' professional involvements; in the long view a laissez-faire attitude in such matters is much more rewarding than a repressive management policy. Such an attitude can be projected by keeping the administrative red tape required for professional participation to a minimum. It can also be projected in a positive sense by sincere recognition of the professional's contributions and achievements from his supervisors and management.

REFERENCES

1. Douglas McGregor, *The Human Side of Enterprise.* New York: McGraw-Hill Book Co., Inc., 1960.
2. Abraham Maslow, "A Theory of Motivation," *Psychological Review*, Vol. 50, 1943, pp. 370–396.
3. F. Herzberg, B. Mausner, and B. Snyderman, *The Motivation to Work*, 2d Ed. New York: John Wiley & Sons, Inc., 1959.
4. F. Herzberg, *Work and the Nature of Man.* Cleveland: World Publishing Co., 1966.

5. R. L. Katz, "Skills of an Effective Administrator," *Harvard Business Review*, September/October 1974, pp. 90–102. Revised and enlarged from author's article of the same title published in *Harvard Business Review*, January/February 1955, pp. 33–42.

6. Robert R. Blake and Jane S. Mouton, *The Managerial Grid*. Houston: Gulf Publishing Co., 1964.

7. P. Hersey and K. H. Blanchard, "Managing Research and Development Personnel: An Application of Leadership Theory," *Research Management*, Vol. 12, No. 5, 1969, pp. 331–338.

8. W. J. Reddin, *Managerial Effectiveness*. New York: McGraw-Hill Book Co., Inc., 1970.

9. J. R. Hinrichs, *High-Talent Personnel: Managing a Critical Resource*. New York: American Management Associations, 1966.

10. L. Meltzer, "Scientific Productivity in Organizational Settings," *Journal of Social Issues*, Vol. 12, No. 2, 1956, pp. 32–40.

11. H. A. Shepard, "Creativity in R/D Teams," *Research & Engineering*, October 1956, pp. 10–13.

12. T. W. Jackson and J. M. Spurlock, *Research and Development Management*. Homewood, Ill.: Dow Jones–Irwin, Inc., 1966.

13. S. L. Spitz, "Satisfactions and Salaries," *Machine Design*, April 1970, pp. 107–111.

14. D. T. Hall and E. E. Lawler, "Job Pressures and Research Performance," *American Scientist*, January/February 1971, pp. 64–73.

15. I. Hirsch, W. Milwitt, and W. J. Oakes, "Increasing the Productivity of Scientists," *Harvard Business Review*, March/April 1958, pp. 66–76.

16. Robert M. Ranftl, "R&D Productivity—A Key Issue," *Astronautics & Aeronautics*, June 1976, pp. 50–56.

17. E. X. Hallenberg, "Dual Advancement Ladder Provides Unique Recognition for the Scientist," *Research Management*, Vol. 13, No. 3, 1970, pp. 221–227.

18. D. Twedt, "Management Handbooks for Continuing Education," *Harvard Business Review*, July/August 1975, pp. 36–38, 40, 44, 46, 161.

19. H. G. Kaufman, "The Graduate Management Degree: Is It Really the Road to Success?" *New Engineer*, February 1974, pp. 29–32, 39–42.

20. P. F. Drucker, *The Practice of Management*. New York: Harper & Row, Publishers, 1954.

21. P. F. Drucker, *Management: Tasks, Responsibilities, Practices*. New York: Harper & Row, Publishers, 1973.

22. Albert Shapiro, "Management of Innovation: The Role of Communication," Sixth International TNO Conference, Rotterdam, March 1-2, 1973. Reprint No. 59, Economics and Business Series, University of Texas, Austin, 1974.

23. William F. Keefe, *Listen, Management!* New York: McGraw-Hill Book Co., Inc., 1971

24. D. C. Pelz, and F. M. Andrews, *Scientists in Organizations.* New York: John Wiley & Sons, Inc., 1966.

25. R. G. Nichols and L. A. Stevens, "Listen to People," in *Business and Industrial Communication, A Source Book,* edited by C. W. Redding and G. A. Sanborn. New York: Harper & Row, Publishers, 1964.

26. M. Dalton and C. Dalton, "Nonverbal Communication in Engineering Teams," *Mechanical Engineering,* December 1975, pp. 12–17.

27. W. D. Garvey and B. E. Compton, "The Flood and How to Survive It," *The Johns Hopkins Magazine,* Fall 1967, pp. 1–12.

28. Robert K. Merton, "Behavior Patterns of Scientists," *American Scientist,* Vol. 57, No. 1, 1969, pp. 1–23.

29. Eric W. Vetter, *Manpower Planning for High Talent Personnel,* Ann Arbor: University of Michigan Press, 1967.

ELEMENTS OF R&D TECHNICAL MARKETING 4

In shallow waters, shrimps make fools of dragons.

The concept of marketing is peculiar to advanced societies of the twentieth century. As nations strive toward higher levels of development of their natural and human resources, they move—almost predictably—through a sequence of steps that determine the way they produce and distribute goods and services. As an aid to understanding what modern technological marketing is, it is worthwhile to review the process first in general terms.

THE MARKETING FUNCTION

The first stage in the evolution of marketing is the production-oriented stage. All emerging societies begin here; some remain in this stage perpetually. It is characterized by the excess of consumer needs over supply, and the first business of business is to produce and distribute essential goods and services in sufficient quantity to meet minimum consumer needs. Variety and choice are subordinated to the higher priority of maintaining and developing the society by supplying the essentials it needs.

The second stage is characterized by a sales orientation of business. Here the production of goods and services has been brought into acceptable balance with need, and greater economic prosperity breeds higher levels of competition. Now that they can supply their goods and services in quantities needed to meet consumer demands, producers must initiate more aggressive sales and distribution practices to maintain their market position. An expanding product base is developed, and the consumer, in effect, is invited to purchase beyond his minimum needs.

The third and final stage is the marketing stage. Here the central problem of management is what to produce. Satisfactory answers to this question can be found only through research of the marketplace, knowledge of changing buyer habits and psychology, and continual change in the product line and services offered. The consumer is courted both by involving him in the planning of new goods and services and by stimulating his interest in buying these products that are largely inessential to his survival. Marketing, then, comprises all efforts directed toward generating markets through the development and distribution of customer-satisfying products and services. As distinguished from sales activities, which tend to be self-serving, marketing is a customer-serving activity.

With the recent emergence of postindustrial society in the United States, this country has, in effect, created the world's first service economy. In 1950, half of all workers were engaged in the production of goods (about one-third directly in manufacturing). Today, almost 65 out of every 100 workers are engaged in services; by 1980, 70 out of every 100 are expected to be employed in service functions; and it has been estimated that by the year 2000 only 10 percent of the labor force will be in manufacturing—producing goods for themselves and the other 90 percent.

As broadly described above, the field of marketing has grown into a significant and complex social science in recent years. It is also distinctively oriented toward production and distribution within segments of the general population—the consumer is here conceived as an individual exercising free choice in the marketplace and assisting industry in defining the goods and services to be produced.

Technical marketing, or the marketing of R&D technology, is just now beginning to emerge as a legitimate area of understanding. There are indeed many differences between conventional and technical marketing practices; but to understand the shape and importance of the latter, it is useful to appreciate the former.

The marketing of technology, after all, is a speciality which draws from general marketing experience; hence it has many of the characteristics of conventional marketing. Before moving on to a closer examination of R&D technological marketing, it is therefore useful to mention a few of the key concepts of marketing which carry over to this new discipline.

Change

In a sense, marketing is synonymous with change, for the marketing concept cannot be carried forward without perpetual change. New products and new services must be made available to a consumer who has a changing appetite. His desire for new products and services is brought on in part by his impatience with the familiar, but more importantly by his curiosity about the new products and services constantly being offered in the competitive marketplace. Also, changes in national mood—brought about by social and economic conflict and by changing life patterns—affect his desire for change. Thus, to ignore the necessity for change is a form of marketing myopia that has caused the demise of many an enterprise.

To meet this constant requirement for change the marketing function must continually create and adapt new products and services, new markets, and new organizational patterns. This can be accomplished only by close monitoring of the consumers' collective pulse. Closely associated with the need for entrepreneural change is *innovation.* Innovation is the process of adapting existing methods or technology to new markets. It differs altogether from *invention,* which refers to the discovery of new methods or technology. The distinction between innovation and invention has been likened to the distinction between engineering and science. The former involves implementing basic known physical principles through an integrated plan that is applied to a new need.

Obsolescence

Another important concept, closely related to marketing innovation, is *obsolescence.* Obsolescence—the process of becoming obsolete or tending toward a state of disuse—comes about either as the result of legitimate functional or design improvements or because product designs have been deliberately planned for a fixed useful life. In the first instance product changes are subject to advance planning only insofar as technology itself can be planned; in the second instance—so-called *planned obsolescence* —superficial style changes or improved functional conveniences are often introduced on a periodic basis so as to render earlier product lines less desirable. Also, durable products or systems are deliberately engineered to have relatively short useful lives, through the use of inferior materials or marginal design.

The subject of obsolescence—particularly planned obsolescence—is highly controversial. Considered within the above framework it is clear that some forms of innovation can in fact be planned or anticipated by industry (as discussed later in this chapter in the section titled "Technological Planning and Forecasting"). Innovation can be programmed into the fabric of the manufacturing industry in such a way as to create a form of planned obsolescence—frequently in anticipation of newer technologies scheduled for adoption in the future. The effect of innovation on planned obsolescence is particularly visible in high-technology industries, such as the computer hardware industry. Another example is found in the Department of Defense, where weapons systems are commonly designed to have a useful life much shorter than is technologically possible; this permits the continuing adoption of new technologies which render existing systems predictably obsolete at an early stage.

In a wider perspective, there are several grounds on which the practice of planned obsolescence is being actively debated. One of these concerns the moral justification for requiring consumers to surrender their purchasing autonomy in the interest of their "social responsibility" to maintain the high levels of consumer expenditures needed to drive the economy ever upward. Another concerns the effect of planned obsolescence on consumer values. Some argue that this practice leads to a fickle and "style conscious" consuming public, whose buying habits are becoming more capricious in response to nonfunctional product changes.

A third and closely related argument concerns the effect of planned obsolescence on our natural resources. There is little doubt that the conspicuous consumption now prevailing in our society has pushed aside other environmental and humanistic priorities. And finally there are implications of the practice in the international economic system. Some maintain that our national economy, in competition with the European Common Market and other multinational cooperatives, must exploit planned obsolescence to remain in the running with these economic systems. Differences arise, of course, in the matter of determining the relative responsibility to place on the producer, on the consumer, and particularly on the government for its increased regulation of industrial practices.

The Organizational Life Cycle

One of the basic principles in marketing economics is the *organizational life cycle*, or the characteristic growth pattern common to all enterprises. This concept is most easily explained with the life cycle diagram, as illustrated in Figure 4-1. As an

Figure 4-1. Life cycle diagram of a typical organization.

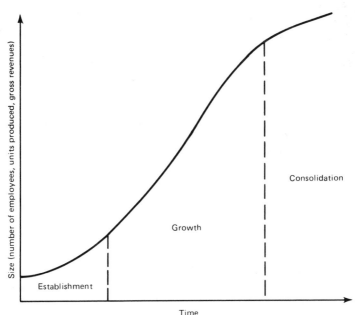

enterprise grows successfully from inception it moves through three distinct regions of growth. Each stage poses special management problems because each stage has its own particular set of objectives.

The first stage—establishment—is characterized by an increasing rate of growth. This "sink or swim" stage commands that management be prudent in cultivating a market and a favorable reputation through specialization and efficient control of resources. In the second stage—the growth stage—the rate of growth is approximately constant. Here, marketing plays its most decisive role in diversifying the product line, opening up new product channels, and projecting a wider reputation. Finally, there is the consolidation stage in which the growth rate decreases and management is concerned primarily with maintaining its market position among the competition. It is here that planned obsolescence can be used most effectively to maintain a rapid turnover of production within a consuming sector of relatively fixed size.

The life cycle function is common to many phenomena in the natural world. The consolidation stage of the life cycle, for example, parallels the emergence of a zero-growth economy. The formulation of effective management goals in the consolidation stage of an enterprise is a challenging task that calls for sound and innovative policies just as in the stages preceding consolidation.

The Product Life Cycle

Closely related to the organizational life cycle is the *product life cycle*. In any industrial organization—high technology or not—organizational longevity depends on the successive creation and development of new products or services, each of which has a characteristic life cycle, as illustrated in Figure 4-2a. As distinguished from an organizational life cycle, which has no foreseeable conclusion, the product life cycle has a finite time scale over which the product is viable. The continuous generation of new products leads to the relationship between the individual product life cycles and their aggregate, the organizational life cycle, as depicted in Figure 4-2b.

Figure 4-2a. Individual product life cycle.

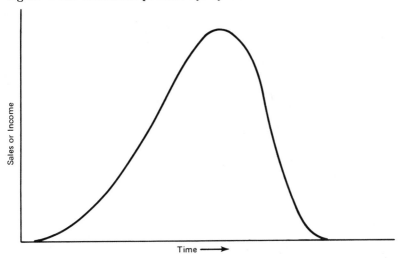

Figure 4-2b. Composition of organizational life cycle in terms of constituent product life cycles.

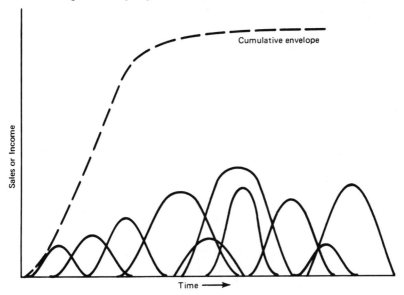

For an organization to develop strongly and exhibit continued technological and financial strength, it must attempt to shorten its product life cycles as well as the intervals between the creation of new products and services. Within the Department of Defense, for example, it takes an average of about eight to ten years for a major system to be brought through its various stages of development; these characteristically are:

Research
Exploratory development
Advanced development
Engineering development
Management support
Operational system development

Interestingly enough, this eight-to-ten-year characteristic time scale has not changed significantly over recent history. It has been estimated, for example, that Orville and Wilbur Wright required eight years and a 7 percent capital investment to initiate the aircraft industry some 70 years ago. However, there is evidence to support the position that DOD systems development cycles take somewhat longer (and corporate investments are higher), on the average, when initiated by an organization than when generated by the government.[1]

Market Planning

Before concluding this section it is appropriate to mention briefly the subject of *planning*. A more detailed discussion of technological planning is presented under the heading "Technological Planning and Forecasting"; however, planning as a management function is important in all types of enterprise. Kelley[2] has described market planning as including

the continuing managerial and technical activities and process involved in assessing areas of marketing opportunity, determining the marketing mission and objectives, developing and coordinating marketing action programs, and evaluating and adjusting all market-related programs. The first two elements of planning are essentially conceptual and analytical; the others are the operational aspects of planning.

Proper planning is vital to the marketing function and should pervade all stages of the firm's life cycle.

In technological marketing, as will be seen, planning assumes a role of critical importance. High-technology product planning has been described as consisting of two components: market analysis and product definition.[3] More than in the case of market forecasting or market research, market analysis includes the implications for product viability of altering the buyer's/user's behavior patterns. It examines in detail the proposed product and specifies the requirements which must be met if it is to be accepted: price, market size and segmentation, and the vulnerability of the market competition. Product definition attempts to combine market analysis with the state of currently available technology. From its initial appearance in conceptual design form, the product moves successively through the stages of detail design, prototype development, and production.

Market planning underlies the whole of the marketing concept, whose principal responsibilities are:

—To program the product/services mix to be offered.
—To create the promotional techniques to be used in offering the products and services.
—To establish the pricing policies.
—To develop the channels of distribution for the products and services.

These four elements form the *marketing mix,* that is, the variables present in the product or service and in the way it is to be sold in the marketplace. The mix can be fine-tuned in various ways to meet particular marketing needs. The mix may be adjusted, for example, through price and promotion strategies to maximize sales of a given consumer product when the market has already been identified. In other situations a market may be created or segmented to respond to new products or services that are offered. The marketing mix concept also applies to organizations undertaking to vary the degree of diversity (or specialization) of services offered to a market. It is this use of the marketing mix that is perhaps most important to technological marketing, as will be brought out in the following sections of this chapter.

TECHNOLOGICAL MARKETING

Technological marketing involves marketing the products and services of advanced technology to commercial and government clients. All the customary aspects of marketing—the product to be marketed, the promotional techniques, the pricing strategy, and the distribution channels—come into play as well in the marketing of high technology as in the marketing of consumer goods. While there are many similarities in the way these various marketing aspects are normally implemented, the differences are more significant. Thus, traditional marketing strategies as applied to consumer products industries often fail to meet the objectives and special requirements of technical marketing.

Before considering some of the more important differences between conventional and technological marketing, it is important to emphasize their common bond: the customer orientation of the marketing concept. Technological marketing is big business. It is highly competitive and subject to the constant pressure of change wrought by technological innovation. Therefore, in order to be successful, all aspects of R&D marketing—as in traditional marketing—must be manifestly customer-oriented. This means that the supplier of high-technology services must constantly interact with his potential marketplace so that innovative, customer-satisfying proposals can be generated. It means that pricing strategies must be tuned to customer requirements so that the level of effort proposed, the schedule that is planned, and the degree of risk to be assumed by the customer will meet his needs. Marketers of high-technology services do themselves a favor in keeping two proven principles always in mind: be customer-oriented and be innovative—and the greater of these is to be customer-oriented.

Among the several distinctions between the effective marketing of high technology and the conventional marketing of consumer products is the relationship between the supplier and his market. The producer of consumer goods normally enjoys the freedom to experiment with his marketplace by making changes in product packaging, in product pricing, and in his distribution channels, that is, by altering the marketing mix. In addition, he may increase his sales and the extent of consumer satisfaction by introducing "tie-ins"—such as service contracts for equipment sold—as well as using other marketing strategies. All these factors can usually be adjusted—in accordance with the marketing feedback he receives—to enhance the product's position. The time frame over which these adjustments can be effectively made is related to the product life cycle, and the product marketing strategy should become relatively stable during the middle and latter stages of the life cycle.

In technological marketing, however, such freedom to experiment with the marketplace is usually not present. More often than not, the supplier of the product or service has but one opportunity to market his proposal to the customer—the customer will buy only once and may choose from a number of competing proposals. Moreover, it is usual for the product or service proposed to be unique in some way, tailored particularly to the customer's requirements and without identical precedent in the seller's prior experience. This "one-shot environment" within which the high-technology marketer must operate places a premium on the seller's knowing exactly what the customer wants and how much he is willing to invest. It is also the factor that makes high-technology marketing distinctively challenging.

Consider the problem of pricing, for example. As compared with more conventional marketing practices where the producer can vary his pricing strategy rather freely,* the high-technology supplier must price his proposal with the knowledge that there usually will be no second chance should his price proposal be judged inferior to those of other proposers.† In the defense industry, for example, there has been a definite trend away from cost-reimbursement contracts in favor of fixed-price contracts. This trend in contracting has resulted in shifting responsibility and risk from the government to the contractor, thus heightening

* Subject, of course, to federal antitrust regulations in certain industries. For example, under the provisions of the Robinson-Patman Act of 1936, price discrimination which cannot be justified on the basis of cost may be held illegal.

† The federal government has begun to use the "best and final offer" practice more frequently in evaluating competitive R&D proposals. This practice, discussed later in the chapter under the heading "R&D Proposals—Evaluation Criteria," allows the leading proposers one opportunity to reevaluate their price offer.

price competition and reducing profits.[1] Commercial organizations seeking to purchase the products of high technology have historically been oriented toward fixed-price contracts, for in this way the customer is purchasing "guaranteed" performance rather than a "best-efforts" performance. As a consequence of this general heightening in price competition within both the government and private sectors, contractors are experiencing greater pressures to employ effective analytical methods for predicting costs and profits.

Another characteristic of high-technology marketing is the range of the products and services being procured. The federal government, for example, procures nearly all the products of technology found in the commercial marketplace as well as a vast spectrum of defense-related services. The defense contractor—even the small, specialized contractor—soon encounters persuasive reasons to broaden his line of services in order to smooth out his contract backlog and take advantage of the many procurements closely related to his principal technology. On the other hand, he is restrained from doing so by his awareness that buyers of high technology are usually members of a very knowledgeable market, and that anything short of demonstrated mastery in his technical proposal or project performance will place him in an unfavorable position. Maintaining objectivity is a most important consideration in the marketing of high technology, and successful contractors soon learn to abide by this principle.

There are, of course, significant differences between government and commercial buyers of high technology, some of which will be brought out later in this chapter. One of the most important distinctions lies in the respective procurement procedures, as discussed in Chapter 5. Government procurement practices tend to be lengthy and cumbersome when compared with the more streamlined commercial practices. In addition, private enterprise has more latitude in restricting competition in its R&D procurements when it appears to be in its own best interests to do so.

Since World War II, government R&D contracting has in fact moved much closer toward a position of encouraging broad competition in its procurements. Prior to that time the available population of contractors competent to produce services of a given kind was small, and so the government necessarily limited its search to those few contractors in whom confidence could be placed. More recently, however, and particularly in the post-Sputnik era, the rapid expansion of R&D capabilities throughout the country has forced the government to broadcast its planned procurements more widely, in the interests of open competition.

There are cases, however, in which unqualified competition in seeking to secure a government contract is undesirable to both sides. Aside from the burden to the sponsoring agency of added evaluation time, the proposal preparation costs are passed along in the form of higher R&D overhead costs which the government must assume in subsequent contract work. Thus there has recently been a trend among certain branches of the federal government, particularly within the DOD, toward placing more restrictions for qualification on prospective contractors prior to bidding.

PROGRAM DEVELOPMENT

The cornerstone of successful R&D marketing lies in program development. The responsibility for developing technical programs rests with both the buyer and the seller. The customer, or user, of advanced technology must constantly coordinate his program with his mission or product line so as to identify those areas where advanced technology must be developed. Once these needs are identified and their timetables established, the requirements for outside contractor assistance can be formulated. This search for contractor support may be a continuous process, or intermittent, as in the case where most technical support is derived internally or where the nature of the business is such that R&D technology support is needed only occasionally.

Moreover, although the customer's search for support is usually an active process, it may be a passive one, as in the case of those branches of the DOD which support basic research. For example, the Office of Naval Research, the Air Force Office of Scientific Research, and the Army Research Office do not gener-

PRINCIPLES OF R&D MANAGEMENT

ally solicit proposals for contract R&D, but rather review incoming proposals with regard to their compatibility with overall mission requirements and budgetary resources.

While the federal government buys technology in support of its various missions, commercial buyers of R&D services are necessarily profit-motivated. This important distinction is often overlooked by contractors. Federal R&D procurements are influenced by cost primarily through budgetary constraints. In addition to being budget conscious, commercial organizations must frequently relate their dollar paid for advanced technology to its probable effect on contribution to profit. As a consequence, the commercial sector is much more limited in its ability to support basic R&D activities, where no direct relation to profit or to a competitive edge may be established.

Marketers of advanced technology services—often themselves in the dual role of buyers—occupy a complementary role in the mutual buyer-seller search. The responsibility falls on the seller to implement the marketing concept by matching his capabilities with the needs of his customers. This is done first by informing prospective customers of his capabilities, and then by tendering formal offers to engage in contract services through the preparation of proposals.

The first of these two steps is basically promotional. It can take several forms but is always directed at identifying potential markets and customers. Many organizations, particularly those of small to medium size, pursue their R&D promotional practices by vesting each individual technical staff member with the responsibility of cultivating markets in his area of expertise. The premise here is that the only person who can successfully sell a research program is the technical person who developed it and who will be responsible for carrying it through.

The technical individual may perform his marketing function in many ways. Among the most effective is through personal contact within the professional circles in which he is active. Attending professional society sessions, writing and delivering papers, and participating in various planning and coordinating panels are all critically important to his mission. These and related promotional activities can bring him the personal contact he needs to cultivate potential customer relationships. Even more important is his need to maintain high levels of confidence with existing sponsors through satisfactory achievement on his present R&D programs.

Some organizations engaging in high-technology services on a larger scale have come to develop separate marketing branches, staffed by competent, broadly based engineers and scientists. The corporate marketing organization interfaces between members of the professional staff—who carry out the technical programs—and the customer. It can compound marketing management problems unless sagaciously implemented. As Professor Divita has explained[5]:

> The concept of selling, as we know it in the classical sense, simply does not apply to the company whose product is R&D. In fact, many of the classical ideas of functions and organizational structure are not found at all in the R&D companies. Experience tells us that salesmen simply cannot sell the capabilities of these companies. Characteristically, they cannot understand the diversity of technologies involved in sufficient depth to convince the customer to buy. So the job of convincing the customer to look favorably on the company's approach has been left to the engineer and the scientist. The salesman has adapted himself to performing two functions: (1) managing the relationship between the customer and the company, and (2) acting as a gatherer of market information. It is not difficult to see that such sharing of the sales function can cause conflict if not properly addressed.

Nevertheless, several large aerospace-related industries have successfully created centralized product management divisions within their corporate structure for the purpose of marketing large, high-technology *systems*. These groups are assigned marketing responsibility for specific systems or broad-based product lines, and operate at their best when in-depth systems knowledge is essential to the marketing task. The marketing manager generally is responsible for establishing goals, preparing and maintaining a marketing plan, coordinating specific cost estimates, coordinating the activities of other functional units on specific products, and providing technical and sales support to technical sales representatives in the company.

The key staff members of the product management units, including the manager, are almost always technically trained engineers or scientists. Customers of high-technology product lines are known to prefer to deal with their technical counterparts in the contracting organizations. The size of these marketing units varies from an office staff of about three (typically with business, engineering, and sales backgrounds) in small to medium-size organizations to a larger division reporting directly to the vice-presidential level in major prime contracting corporations.

Centralized marketing units as described above generally have not been as successful in representing narrow R&D services as in promoting large, technically complex systems in the aerospace, computer, and comparable fields. For this reason, centralized marketing groups may give assistance to, but do not take over, the marketing responsibility for small R&D contracts. This responsibility is better vested in the technical staff designated to perform the work.

R&D PROPOSALS—THE BID DECISION

One aspect of the proposal process that is frequently given less attention than it deserves is the decision whether or not to bid on a solicited procurement. The subject of bid strategy has undergone a considerable transformation in the years following World War II. At that time, the number of firms known to be technically qualified to respond to advanced R&D bid invitations was quite small by today's standards. Bid invitations—called also in the trade RFPs (requests for proposals), RFQs (requests for quotations), IFBs (invitations for bids), or PRs (purchase requests)—were sent to a small, selected group of firms, with competition intentionally limited. However, as technology continued to expand and many new firms emerged as equally qualified, this policy came under attack. The result was that the policy was changed, and bid invitations began to be sent out much less selectively, in the name of fair and free competition.

This evolution in procurement policy has brought about changes in the bidding strategy employed today by R&D firms. In earlier days, when competition was more limited, one's statistical chances of a successful bid were high, and bid requests usually were subject to little screening by the prospective bidder, provided the project offered for bid was in the firm's area of experience and capability. Furthermore, once a contract was secured, the possibility of additional follow-on contract work with the same sponsor was common practice.

Today, however, increased competition among contractors has made the situation quite different. Bid requests often are distributed on a relatively unrestricted basis, and the number of firms responding to a given bid request may be very large. This not only reduces one's statistical chances of success but—according to some observers—introduces an additional dimension of randomness in the evaluation. Because of human limitations in the evaluation process, the ranking of proposals by quality may not be as objective as when only a few proposals are being reviewed. In view of these factors a firm often must make the agonizing decision to "no-bid" an invitation despite the fact that the effort being solicited is in the sphere of experience and capability of the firm.

Other factors may be present, of course, and these may override a seemingly obvious decision to bid. More and more, R&D industries engaged in competitive bidding for government contracts must carefully screen incoming bid invitations and be more selective in choosing those on which to bid. Thus the bid decision itself is not unlike the proverbial tail that wags the dog. The quality of the bid/no-bid decision, while requiring only a small cost investment, directly controls a heavy commitment of cost effort necessary to prepare the proposal, and indirectly affects the risk posture of the firm in bidding on contracts.

Thus the importance of making a timely and judicious bid/no-bid decision can hardly be overemphasized. In many instances the lead time available for proposal preparation is short, and delay in reaching a bid/no-bid decision can seriously compromise the quality of the proposal.

Figure 4-3 identifies those elements considered to be most important in reaching the bid decision. Under this breakdown, the decision problem is to be viewed distinctly from the standpoint of the bidding organization and from the organiza-

Figure 4-3.   Elements in the bid/no-bid decision.

CONTRACTOR'S POSITION

Technical elements
Is area of genuine interest?
Does sponsor recognize problem area and place priority on
its solution?
Have we an established reputation in area?
Have we worked previously for same group?
Have we coordinated thoroughly with sponsor on problem
area?
Do we have all facilities expected of successful contractor?
Is our risk exposure concerning our proprietary ideas
acceptable?

Economic elements
Is contract amount in line with proposal preparation costs?
Is sponsor known to have already committed requisite
funds?
Is any competitor known to have an inside track on this
job?
Is anticipated gross fee (profit) acceptable?
Is contract type acceptable?
Would contract award likely lead to follow-on contracts?
Do expected quality and number of competitors constitute
acceptable risk level?

Strategic elements
Is program consistent with company plans and objectives?
Is there adequate lead time to write proposal?
Are requisite people available to assist in proposal prep-
aration?
Are supporting facilities and services available?
Can internal communications be established effectively?

SPONSOR'S EXPECTED EVALUATION

Technical elements
Quality, soundness, and originality of proposal
Understanding and appreciation of problem
Prior technical performance
Reputation of principal investigator(s)
Reputation of company
Possession of needed capabilities and facilities

Economic elements
Company cost structure
Prior financial performance
Capability to do job on time at cost

tion's evaluation of the sponsor's position. Under the contractor's position, for example, three major elements have been identified: technical, economic, and strategic. Each of these can be more finely divided in turn into a number of specific considerations, posed as questions which must be answered subjectively (but candidly) by the potential bidder. The checklist also calls for the contractor's best guess as to how the sponsor will react to the proposal. Again, several considerations are named, and these must be answered as objectively as possible.

Most organizations seriously engaged in contract R&D technology agree that assessment of competitive strength is one of the most important elements in making an objective decision on whether or not to bid. In solicited bid requests, for example, those firms not present on the original bidder's list—although they are perhaps in a position to establish their qualifications and thus receive a bid invitation—are likely to be facing strong statistical odds. In assessing competitive strength, Soelberg[6] describes

> . . . evidence that a bidding company needs to get in there well before the official invitation to bid on a contract has left the government agency—that at this time one can predict with disturbing success which firm will get the contract, simply by looking at the order of names on the list of those invited to bid.

Successful bidders are usually those companies which have had sufficient coordination with the R&D procurement initiator to be placed first or second, or perhaps third, on the suggested source list.

Several organizations have found it useful to develop *bid/no-bid rating sheets* consisting of a series of questions similar to those in Figure 4-3 to be answered by the key person(s) responsible for the decision. In some cases the completed sheet is graded "objectively" in an effort to quantify the process. Perhaps the most important benefit of such a procedure, once it is accepted and used, is to influence the persons involved to think through all steps in the decision process in a rational and objective way before reaching a firm decision.

There may be reasons for deciding to bid on a given invitation other than those indicated by the analysis described above. For example, many firms on occasion have decided to "buy into" a technology by cost sharing, that is, by underwriting part of the expected costs. This is done in anticipation of the probability that the reduced cost to the buyer will outweigh deficiencies or other factors, so that the contractor will be able to enter a new phase of technology that promises to be fruitful to him in the long run. The buying-in strategy often does partially mitigate other weaknesses in the proposal. Nevertheless, it should be done only after a careful and objective appraisal of both the solicitation in question and the likely bid position of later solicitations in the same technological area. Also, the federal government is restricted from awarding contracts to firms offering to cost-share if the sole reason for the award is willingness to cost-share.

Having thus far emphasized a rational approach to decision making, it is of interest to outline briefly the radically distinct approach of Bjorksten[7] based on game theory analysis. This approach rests essentially on two propositions:

> When a large number of bidders (say, ten or more) respond to a bid invitation, an element of chance is introduced into the reviewing procedure which makes it unlikely that the proposals will be ranked with a high degree of rationality.

> When, owing to a high bidder response, the review procedure lacks rationality, it is unrewarding to spend more time preparing a proposal than is necessary to be fully responsive.

If one accepts these two propositions (and most persons probably will not), it follows that in examining all bid requests that are likely to bring a large number of responses, one may base his bidding strategy on a process of random selection. In the case of the Bjorksten Research Laboratories[7]:

> Answering 1 invitation to bid out of every 12 received is sufficient to remain active in the mainstream of development information, providing that the replies are spread randomly. Therefore, the best game appears to be to answer every twelfth invitation to bid by sequence, *regardless of the subject or of the bidders' interests or qualifications*, as long as a passable job could be done in case of award. Giving preference to invitations in an area of special competence would result in an unnecessary concentration of bids in that area and a thinning out in other areas to the point of being

dropped out in these. The loss in information flow from the other areas would more than offset the somewhat better yield of contracts in the area of concentration.

This interesting theory has yet to be applied in an operating management framework. While no one (least of all, this author) is an advocate of this process, it does stress the caution needed in responding to bid invitations widely broadcast.

In developing policy or guidelines for bidding decisions, it is of great interest to examine the distinctions in proposal activity among "winning" and "losing" firms. Analyzing the results of 1,100 companies solicited by the federal government to bid on 45 R&D award competitions, Roberts[8] drew the following conclusions:

—Winners had done far more prior contractual work with the government agency.
—Winners had submitted more prior unsolicited proposals.
—Winners did not think the procurement belonged to someone else.
—Winners did frequently think the procurement tended to belong to them.
—Winners knew the technical initiator.
—Winners contacted the initiator after receiving the RFPs but before submitting their proposals.
—Winners felt they had an advantage over their competition.
—Winners reflected customer technical preferences in their proposals.
—Winners directed their proposals at particular individuals in the organization.
—Winners made minimum use of technical writers in the preparation of their proposals.

All these characteristics were statistically significant in that losers evidenced opposite characteristics. A key finding of the analysis was that all meaningful differences between winning and losing companies were identified with activity *preceding* RFP receipt. In terms of activities, strategies, and decisions following receipt of the RFP, Roberts found no factor that led to a significant distinction between high-performing and low-performing companies. These conclusions fortify the importance of a marketing (contact) orientation toward R&D as distinguished from a sales (proposal) orientation.

R&D PROPOSALS—PREPARATION

Proposal formats vary widely in organization, length, style, and emphasis, depending on what the authors perceive as the most effective combination for the procurement being sought. Despite the wide differences found among successful proposals, most share a common set of elements. Taken together, these elements attempt to demonstrate forthrightly why this proposal in particular offers a program of superior quality in solving the problems of interest to the sponsor. The overriding themes of the proposal should always be technical mastery and honesty. Without these two ingredients the proposal has scant chance of success; or in the event of contract award, the ensuing technical program is destined to be plagued with difficulties.

Nearly every proposal concerned with high technology contains six elements[9]:

Proposal summary
Statement of the problem
Technical proposal
Management plan
Facilities and related experience
Cost proposal

Sometimes these basic elements are divided or recombined in various ways. Nevertheless, in one form or another they should be present in nearly every proposal; they therefore constitute the basis for the ensuing discussion of effective proposals.

Proposal Summary

The proposal summary is one of the most vital of all proposal elements since it certainly will be read by everyone who evaluates the proposal, and may indeed be the *only* section read by those administrators who have ultimate authority over its disposition. This lead section of the proposal should summarize succinctly all the remaining elements* of the proposal in a brief,

* Except for the cost data in cases where the cost proposal is to be submitted as a document separate from the technical proposal.

persuasive, and clear prose style. In a few hundred words it should present an understanding of the essence of the problem, the proposed solution stated in broad terms, the essentials of the management plan, and a statement concerning the strength of the background being brought to the program as well as any unique facilities to be employed. Within the bounds of simple honesty, the proposal summary should emphasize the special assets of the proposal—well-qualified program participants, unique approaches and facilities, competitive strengths, and so forth—and what these assets will mean to the program. This section should attempt to leave the reader with a premonition that this proposal may likely prove to be the obvious choice.

Statement of the Problem

Before presenting the details of the solution it is important to put forth a clear statement of the problem being addressed. One important guide to this section—in the case of solicited proposals—is the request for proposal itself, although in some instances the technical problem as defined therein is so vague or poorly conceived as to be of limited use. Thus, as a rule this section should present a clear statement of the problem in the proposer's own words, clarifying ambiguities in the RFP, and bringing out ancilliary problems that may be anticipated. Exceptions to the problem definition as developed in the work statement should be brought out and supporting reasons given. Indeed, if no exceptions to the work statement are anticipated, this fact should likewise be clearly stated.

There are three general guidelines that are often helpful in developing this section of the proposal. First, it should be brief relative to the section which spells out the detailed technical proposal. Second, it should communicate a sound awareness of the need the sponsoring organization has for the procurement, particularly insofar as interfaces between this and related programs and technologies are concerned. This means that the proper perspective of the program should be understood, and how the end product is related to the customer's overall needs and his own achievements in the technology. Finally, it should be borne in mind that the statement of the problem is distinct from its solution. This portion of the proposal should set the stage for the proposed approach, but not anticipate it.

Technical Proposal

With rare exceptions the technical proposal is the most important single section of any R&D proposal in terms of the weight given it in the evaluation process. It is also the most unique; therefore in each new proposal the style and content of this section may be expected to depart considerably from those of earlier proposals. Nevertheless, there are certain guidelines that experience has shown to be useful in preparing this section, the heart of any proposal.

The objective of the technical proposal section is to *sell* the proposal. To do this it is essential to know and understand the overall needs of the customer. If he is looking for a prototype development using off-the-shelf components, don't try to sell him a concept with high originality and components that must first be developed. The proposal should be keyed to the customer's needs so that it can stress the advantages to him of buying this particular proposal.

The overall organization of this section is often effectively done in "sandwich style." The heart of the section should be preceded and concluded by tightly written summaries telling the reader what he is about to be told and what he has just been told, respectively. The style throughout should be clear and unsophisticated, yet uncompromisingly complete. This can often be accomplished by placing some necessary detail in an appendix, to facilitate reading by all interested parties. Graphics should be inserted where they can easily summarize or integrate information whose verbal description may be long or complex. Graphics should be kept simple—to the point where readers with limited time or background can grasp the essential ideas easily without reading through the section in detail.

It is also an effective practice in many proposals to include a brief mention of anticipated problem areas. Surely the informed customer will not be blind to these, and bringing them out into the open can add a dimension of sincerity and awareness. The

Table 4-1.   Guide to content of technical proposal.

Topics Addressed in Technical Proposal	Study	Study, Development, and Production	Development and Production	Hardware
Introduction	X	X	X	X
Study tasks (technical approach, solution, data presentation)	X	X		
Preliminary systems design		X	X	
Final systems design—operational equipment		X	X	
Functional description (capabilities)		X	X	
Prototype development (fabrication, test, reliability)		X	X	
Production				X
Reliability/quality control				X
Checkout—debugging and maintenance				X
Operation—training				X
Deliverable items—reports, software, equipment, installation, test, checkout, training	X	X	X	X
Summary	X	X	X	X

customer should be assured, however, that his risk position is minimized through intelligent program planning, and because, as the buyer, he has ultimate control over execution of the project.

Table 4-1 presents some general guidelines as to the content of the technical proposal section. How the proposal is organized in each particular case will depend on the customer's requirements as perceived by the proposal writers. The entire section should be so packaged as to present a clear and complete message to the sponsor. In addition, aggressive persuasiveness should permeate the presentation; after all, the customer must be convinced of the superiority of this particular proposal over all competitors—all of whom, it must be assumed, also offer to give him what he wants.

Management Plan

Formerly an element of secondary interest, the management plan has recently been given a stature of major importance in R&D proposals. The reasons for this are several: increased sensitivity to cost and schedule slippages, the increasingly complex systems nature of many procurements, and the generally higher levels of technical competition among equally qualified bidders. Therefore, the prudent proposal writer will give this section of the proposal the full attention it deserves, and not simply paste together "boiler-plate" material drawn from earlier proposals, except where such material is clearly relevant and up to date.

The management plan should lead the reader easily from the general to the specific organizational system. It should usually begin with a brief statement of the overall organizational structure, including size, fiscal indices, major functional units, and subsidiaries. Then the major functional unit(s) involved in the proposed program should be described in terms of mission, management, and lines of coordination.

This brief background having been established, considerably more emphasis should be given to the specific project team management being proposed. The project manager should be identified, and his professional profile, together with those of other key project members (including outside consultants), should be included; these profiles should be composed with an eye to their relevance to the particular project requirements. The project team's discussion should clearly show who the customer's point of contact is and where the real authority lies for decisions affecting the project.

Project organization charts or other graphics should be constructed to show both the lines of coordination connecting all participating cost/profit centers and the communications channels connecting the contractor with the sponsor and other outside units involved, including subcontractors. As in preceding proposal sections, innovation and salesmanship should be woven into the fabric of the presentation to catch the customer's interest and convince him of the benefits the program will realize from this well-planned management approach.

There are many ways besides the use of effective graphics to accomplish these purposes. For example, a signed letter from the chief executive officer stating his personal interest and responsibility in the program is both appropriate and effective where relatively large projects are involved. Likewise, photographs of key project team members in conjunction with biographical information can link their responsibilities with their professional accomplishments and so leave a more lasting mental impression with the proposal evaluators.

The management plan should also include—and frequently *must* include—schedules that relate time, work effort levels, and tasks. A timetable showing the relative start-up and completion of each program task should be shown, and assurances given (backed up by historical data on similar programs, where possible) that the schedule can and will be met. The cost basis for each program task should also be given. In many federal procurements, the cost proposal must be submitted as a separate attachment to the main technical proposal for reasons of independent evaluation. In these cases, man-hour allocations should be used in lieu of actual program costs. In the event that a PERT or other critical path management planning system is to be used, this system and its interaction with the proposed program should be described in adequate detail. Finally, any other information involving the program management function should be included, such as agreements with subcontractors, travel, purchased items and capital equipment, vendors employed, and security requirements.

Facilities and Related Experience

Having now thoroughly convinced the customer that the bidder knows what is wanted and how it can best be achieved, it remains to convince the buyer of one other highly important qualification—experience. Part of this qualification lies in special hardware and equipment that have been developed and used on previous projects and are relevant to the program. They may include testing facilities, manufacturing capabilities, quality control and nondestructive evaluation equipment, and production processing facilities. Emphasis should be given to the relevant—and particularly to the unique—capabilities. While it is tempting to include boiler-plate descriptions of general facilities, this should be generally avoided on the premise that all other qualified bidders likewise have similar equipment, so why dilute what's important with what's presumed?

The customer will be interested in knowing all he can of past contract work closely related to the proposed program. Previous and current programs that are relevant should be described briefly, stressing positive accomplishments (both technical and managerial). For purposes of easy identification these program briefs should be augmented with sponsor identification, contract numbers, dates, and costs. Where appropriate, this same kind of information should be supplied on behalf of participating subcontractors.

The objective of this information is to demonstrate to the customer (if possible) that the proposal fits naturally into the bidder's business activities, that the proposer has successfully completed similar projects, and that these related projects have enhanced his understanding of the needs, problems, and procedures peculiar to the buyer's program. As elsewhere in the proposal, graphics should be used where they can effectively show similar results from research efforts and hardware developments, or where they can describe capabilities.

Cost Proposal

The cost proposal may be as simple as a single cost quotation or as complex as a detailed financial proposal, by program task, based on audited direct and indirect costs. It is the usual practice of federal procurement agencies to require detailed cost proposals of the latter type, whereas commercial customers usually have less stringent requirements. The level of detail, however, ultimately depends on the procuring organization, the contract type, and the program complexity. The cost proposal is often required to be submitted as a separate attachment to the technical proposal in order that each may be evaluated on an independent basis.

The cost proposal should be reviewed by a contracting officer of the bidding organization, a staff specialist who is experienced in preparing cost forms and in the accounting procedures used. The cost proposal must be signed by an authorized officer of the organization in order to make the offer legally binding on acceptance. The cost value of the proposed program may or may not be stated or implied in the RFP solicitation. In the event that it is not, and frequently in other cases as well, a management decision on the cost value of the program may be in order. This decision must be made in the face of what is known of the anticipated costs, the customer's needs, the level of competition, and the balance between risks taken and expected payoffs.

Once this decision or set of guidelines has been set, the distribution of costs is computed across all program tasks, commensurate with the total program value. This procedure is sometimes referred to as the *top-down* costing process. It is used to cost programs concerned primarily with basic or exploratory R&D, where program objectives tend to be more general and can therefore be satisfied with varying completeness at several levels of technical effort. In the case of procurements of a more specific nature, especially where hardware or production units are involved, program costing is usually accomplished by the *bottom-up* process. Here, program costs are computed from the specific tasks required, and the total program value represents the sum of the component costs. In addition to the cost process used (top down, bottom up, or a combination of both), final program costs will also account for assumed risk based on the type of contract proposed.

The cost portion of the proposal should state the contract type, terms, and conditions. These items frequently are presented as requirements or recommendations in the RFP. The cost proposal should also convince the buyer that the proposed costs are fair and reasonable. In general, where cost negotiations are anticipated in the event of contract award, the bidder should strive to include as complete a cost basis as possible. To do less may weaken his hand at the negotiation table. This means not only that man-hours and direct and indirect costs be specified, but also that cost incentives, burden and labor rates, general overhead, and fee rates be provided. Where subcontractors or consultants are involved, their costs should be based on firm estimates or quotes where possible. Materials, supplies, travel, and other project expenses likewise should be itemized to complete the cost basis. Finally, it is important to ensure that all cost format requirements of the customer have been complied with.

A word should be added here with regard to cost sharing. Occasionally it is in the interest of the bidding organization to offer to share direct labor or facilities acquisition costs in order to render its proposal more attractive. This may be effective when the proposal may be considered otherwise noncompetitive owing to inadequate experience, contention with "name" organizations in the field, buyer insistence on cost sharing, or other factors.

This practice can be rationalized in only two ways. It may be considered a loss leader in the sense that award of the program will be an entrée into much more work of a related nature in the future—work that otherwise may be inaccessable to the bidding organization. On the other hand, this practice can sometimes be justified on the economic grounds that when the workload is down it is better to cover some of the fixed operating costs through a cost-sharing arrangement than to have staff with no work to do. Regardless of the motivation, however, it should be borne in mind that federal procurement policies forbid awards in which willingness to share costs is the sole basis for the award.

R&D PROPOSALS—EVALUATION CRITERIA

Beginning in the early 1950s, both federal and commercial organizations undertook to refine and improve their proposal evaluation procedures. As a result of these efforts, present procurement practices tend to be more open and objective than formerly. Department of Defense procurement practices currently are governed by the Armed Services Procurement Regulations (ASPR), which spell out in detail the basic rules for evaluating R&D proposals. Similar regulations have been promulgated by NASA, ERDA, DOT, and NSF; these are described in Chapter 5. Many of the major high-technology corporations that buy R&D in support of their missions have developed procurement guidelines paralleling those of the federal government with a view toward ensuring uniformity and fairness in their own proposal evaluations.

In nearly any solicitation where a technical proposal is involved, the paramount factors in evaluating the proposal are (1) a full understanding of the problem to be solved. (2) demonstration of a carefully thought out approach which shows signs of promise if executed as described, and (3) a project team sufficiently skilled and experienced to engender confidence that the project will be successful.

Certainly, proposals developing innovative or revolutionary ideas which offer the likelihood of significant technological breakthroughs are judged with great interest in the R&D market. However, proposals describing the application of well-established approaches can be evaluated favorably if the reasons for failure of prior application of the approaches are analyzed, adequately investigated, and a new and promising solution proposed. In addition to demonstrating an understanding of the problem and an attractive solution for solving it, it is important that the proposal convey the contractor's clear understanding of the mission and the needs of the agency or organization to which the proposal has been submitted.

In many cases the technical and cost portions of the proposal are evaluated separately by respective teams of specialists. This is commonplace with proposals written in response to a formal advertised solicitation. The purpose of this procedure is to ensure that the technical evaluation, which is the most important in the evaluation process, is done impartially with respect to cost information.

Some procurement offices have developed standardized checklists for quantitative ranking of proposals. These checklists vary from customer to customer, and may be set aside when a large and complex procurement suggests that a more comprehensive evaluation form be drawn up for that particular situation. In general, however, most evaluation checklists for nonhardware technical proposals follow a pattern similar to that shown in Figure 4-4. The weighting criteria to be used in the ranking procedure are developed prior to the evaluation by the evaluation committee. In some cases this committee may be a pair of individuals, whereas in more complex procurements the committee may consist of several members of each of the specific areas to be evaluated. Nearly every area of evaluation is at least partially subjective, so that judgment must be exercised together with as much objectivity as possible.

In the case of advertised multisource procurements, immediately following the proposal acceptance deadline (which is usually firm, but in some cases may be flexible), the evaluation committee is convened to begin its work. The technical proposals are evaluated, ranked, and divided into two broad categories: acceptable and nonacceptable. In the case of gov-

Figure 4-4. Typical technical proposal evaluation form.

```
  1.  Scientific/Engineering Approach
      A.  Understanding of the problem        _____
      B.  Soundness of approach               _____
      C.  Compliance with requirements        _____
      D.  Special technical factors           _____
                                  Subtotal              _____
  2.  Procuring Agency's Experience with Contractor
      A.  Technical quality                   _____
      B.  Quality of product or service       _____
      C.  Overrun history                     _____
      D.  Ability to meet schedules           _____
                                  Subtotal              _____
  3.  Qualifications Based on Data Submitted
      A.  Specific experience                 _____
      B.  Special technical equipment/facilities  _____
      C.  Analytical capability               _____
      D.  Technical organization              _____
                                  Subtotal              _____
                                  Grand Total           _____
```

ernment procurements, as with those of many larger commercial organizations, specific reasons for acceptability and nonacceptability must be entered into the procurement record for future reference. Only after the technical evaluation process has been completed can the cost data be brought in for consideration. Of those technical proposals judged acceptable, the lowest cost bid is usually selected for procurement. Sometimes, however, when large cost differences are involved or when strong subjective factors are present, a decision may be made to negotiate with someone other than the lowest cost bidder.

An exception to this customary practice has emerged recently within certain federal agencies, some of which have implemented a "best and final offer" procedure wherein each of the organizations whose proposals have survived to the last stage of evaluation are asked to quote their final price, with or without a change in work scope. Frequently, but not always, the implication to the bidder is that costs must somehow be cut across the board. This practice has been criticized on the assumption that any resulting cost saving is specious, and that the built-in competition among bidders ensures that costs will be as realistic as possible. It has yet to be proved that the practice has resulted in actual cost savings; indeed, it has frequently encouraged cost and schedule overruns.

When the successful bidder has been announced—usually after the negotiations have been culminated—each bidder normally is entitled to a debriefing. It is important that all bidding organizations, winners and losers alike, avail themselves of this valuable right, for it is the only source of feedback on which to build an "experience bank" for future proposal efforts. For example, such feedback can indicate the fact and reasons for noncompetitiveness in a particular market—valuable pieces of information for management.

The debriefing is most effectively approached by an informal meeting, conducted with the constructive attitude of gathering information for the betterment of future proposal efforts. During the debriefing meeting, the specific reasons for losing (or winning!) should be ascertained. Among the questions the bidder should ask are these: How did my price compare with that of my

competition? How many bids were submitted? What were the
ranking criteria, and where did my proposal stand in the ranking? What were the strong and weak points of my proposal, and
how could it have been improved? Finally, and most importantly, the information gathered at the debriefing should be dissemi-
nated to all technical and management persons involved in the
proposal preparation.

TECHNOLOGICAL PLANNING AND FORECASTING

Planning is the conscious effort to select the best course of
action from among various perceived alternatives in order to accomplish a future objective. As was mentioned earlier in this
chapter in the section titled "The Marketing Function," planning is a management function of considerable importance to all
organizations. Technological planning is the process of planning
as applied to high-technology enterprises. It addresses the need
to anticipate or forecast probable directions of technological
development.

This need may arise from the continuing requirement to push
current technology boundaries further into undeveloped areas
either for competitive reasons or for the successful management
of large, long-range projects whose completion and marketability
depend on the development of new technology. Usually, both
motives are present on a more or less continuing basis. In recent
years certain techniques have emerged which are peculiar to the
technological planning process, and these are being used on an
ever expanding scale to cope with the need to forecast into an
uncertain future environment.

Approaches to Forecasting

Some planning techniques are classified as *reactive*. These
approaches to the planning process view the social, economic,
political, and technological forces at work in our human environment as inevitable; thus, if correctly interpreted, they can be
used to predict future trends. The reactive approach corresponds
to the *ontological* view of nature, where naturally evolving systems are studied from the vantage point of an observer. By

trained observation and systematic data gathering, the careful observer can draw certain conclusions regarding the probable future course of technology.

Other planning strategies are called *formative*. This type of planning conceives of the future as being at least partially susceptible to man's efforts to mold current technology. According to this view, formulating and implementing plans will influence the fulfillment of future objectives—if only to a limited extent. The formative approach is aligned with the *teleological* view that science and technology are shaped by man's influence on social, political, economic, and other environmental factors. Thus, according to this view, technology is seen as a byproduct of society. Technological planning processes usually include both reactive and formative elements. Plans must be made in recognition not only of certain trends over which an organization has no sensible influence but also of that technology over which the organization expects to have some control.

Certainly one of the most important aspects of technological planning is that of *technological forecasting* (TF). TF consists of various quantitative techniques that have been developed to predict the short-term course of technology. It has been defined as[10]

> . . . quantified predictions of the timing and of the character of the degree of change of technical parameters and attributes associated with the design, production, and use of devices, materials, and processes according to a specified system of reasoning.

Thus, TF is a systematic method or set of methods for using information (scientific or otherwise) to make quantitative predictions regarding future technology.

Before discussing some of the techniques that are used in technological forecasting, it is important to draw a distinction between TF and planning. TF differs from planning in that TF does not imply a commitment to allocate resources. It may include an analysis of the resources needed to achieve the capabilities projected, but the decision to allocate resources belongs to the planning process. Planning also involves estimates of available resources and the benefits to be gained from fulfilling the technology forecast. That is, management, as part of its planning function, must translate the TF information into the goals, policies, programs, and procedures which will guide the course of the organization.[11]

One of the two main branches of TF is an activity known as *exploratory forecasting*. Here the approach is to extrapolate into the future from known historical and current technological developments. A major branch of exploratory forecasting is *intuitive forecasting;* in its simplest form intuitive forecasting is based on a person's best subjective judgment of the shape of a future state of technology. One of the more reliable intuitive forecasting methods is known as the *Delphi method,* developed by the RAND Corporation in the late 1960s. Here a panel of experts— all of whom are mutually anonymous—address a forecasting problem through a questionnaire process administered through the mails by a single coordinator. After the first questionnaire return is analyzed by the coordinator, the summary returns are given to panel participants, who may then modify their forecasts. The iteration process may be repeated more than once until a stable set of conclusions emerges. For all its obvious strengths, the Delphi method suffers from being expensive, time-consuming, and tainted by peer influence.

Another approach to exploratory forecasting is *trend analysis.* The techniques here may consist of curve fitting or simple mathematical extrapolations of leading and lagging technology trends to predict the future. Projections are also made by statistical correlation techniques, sometimes in connection with mathematical models. Regardless of the kind of extrapolation made, however, trend analysis is highly judgmental in character; it relies on the choice of trend indices, the choice of scale, the constraints chosen, and the way in which nonlinear growth in technological developments is modeled.

The second of the two main branches of TF is known as *normative forecasting.* In contrast to exploratory forecasting, this approach attempts to make present or near-term technology forecasts based on future needs. The philosophy here is that technology will rise to fill the needs created by society.

Among the techniques used in normative forecasting is so-called *morphological analysis.*[12] In this procedure a matrix is constructed in which all conceivable combinations of technological approaches and configurations to solve a given problem are analyzed. An intelligent evaluation of the matrix combinations then reveals various promising approaches which otherwise may have been overlooked. But like so many others, this technique is weak in that it relies so heavily on the judgment of the person who constructs and analyzes the matrix.

Another technique sometimes used is known as the *relevance tree*. The approach here is to lay out a detailed hierarchy of all the paths which can possibly lead to a technological objective. At each level, the sum of the entries at the immediately preceding level should contain a complete set of the information needed to characterize the given level. The purpose in constructing a relevance tree is to divide the process leading from conception to completion into manageable segments, thereby permitting an organized study of those levels in which areas needing improvement or upgrading are discovered. Industrial organizations using relevance trees as a TF tool usually assign weighting criteria at each level to assist in determining which elements at a given level must be improved to support the needs of the next-higher level.

The *mission flow diagram* is another tool of morphological analysis; it resembles the relevance tree in many respects, but is applied in the reverse sense. Instead of outlining all possible paths leading to an end result, the mission flow diagram maps out all possible contingencies resulting from a sequence of decisions. Mission flow analysis defines the alternative policies, responses, and supporting technology needed for major future developments. With this tool the analyst attempts to identify the most useful technology for future investment. At the present time, mission flow analysis is costly and not as widely used as other techniques, but it remains valuable in that it reveals alternative and "best" ways to perform a mission.

These are just some of the TF techniques that have been developed recently to aid in technology planning. Other methods include scenarios—made famous by Herman Kahn—and methods borrowed from the field of operations analysis. All these methods are potentially useful in helping to plan for an uncertain future by identifying promising opportunities and un-covering market implications of changes in technology.

TF has its limitations, however. It is much better suited to predicting evolutionary developments than breakthroughs, for example. Also, its results are apt to be strongly influenced by changes in society's value systems; such changes cannot at present be reliably accounted for by using TF methods. As with any other quantitative tool, the result is subject to the quality of the input. Often in making a technological forecast the analyst is limited by incomplete data and must rely on judgmental inputs that are subject to human interpretation. These factors certainly tend to weaken the credibility of such forecasts.

Because of these inherent limitations now present in its methods, TF has met with some resistance from corporate planners. There is general skepticism about man's ability to predict or manipulate the future, and hence reticence to translate TFs into active planning. Also, there is undoubtedly an uneasy feeling on the part of management that rigorous forecasting methods may bring to light past decisions that were poorly conceived.[13]

Before TF can become more widely accepted as a management planning tool, managers will need to be better informed as to the feasibility of using TF in their own organizational environment. To achieve this, middle- and upper-level management must be adequately exposed to planning and forecasting activities. Only then can managers appreciate the role of TF as a methodology which can bring together complex environmental influences in a way that will suggest optimal future strategies. Moreover, management must appreciate the implications of TF as applied to specific company planning problems, including the threats and opportunities such forecasts may reveal. Finally, if forecasts are to receive acceptance for their potential support of the planning/decision process, they must be available when management needs them.[14] Unless TF tools can be applied in areas of change that can be specifically and directly related to the critical undertakings and objectives of the organization, they have no place. If this pragmatic orientation is absent, TF purposes are better served by informal monitoring and scanning of the technological environment.

Critical Path Methods in Program Management

This discussion would not be complete without an examination of the *critical path method* (CPM) developed in 1957 and the related network approaches to program planning and management. These approaches differ from the TF methods just discussed in that they consider the most efficient ways to plan for and manage program elements once the beginning point and the end objectives have been clearly defined. Although CPM methods are normally considered as management control techniques, they have proved to be quite useful in planning large and complex technical projects.

Among federal agencies, the most widely accepted of the CPM methods for technical project planning and management is the *Program Evaluation and Review Technique* (PERT). This was created by the Navy in response to its need to manage the development of the Polaris weapon system both efficiently and in a condensed time schedule.

The first step in constructing a PERT network analysis is to define the ultimate objective and all the major milestones that must be met in reaching the program objective. These milestones are then linked together in a flow network consisting of circles—called events—connected by arrows indicating the direction of the activity between successive events. Each activity has a beginning and end point (events), and these activities may be performed in series or parallel, as dictated by the nature of the project.

Next, PERT requires that three time estimates be associated with the completion of each activity: t_o, the most optimistic (shortest), t_m, the most likely, and t_p, the most pessimistic (longest). The expected time to complete an activity between two successive events is calculated from these estimates by use of the formula $t_E = \frac{1}{6}(t_o + 4t_m + t_p)$. This network plan can then be analyzed by linear programming computer methods to determine the most time-consuming path of the many that connect program initiation and completion. This information then serves as a management flag to suggest reallocation of resources or other means of reducing this critical path, thus improving overall program performance.

Figure 4-5 gives a simple illustration of a PERT network[15] for a project consisting of 15 events. The boldface arrows in this example describe the critical path, over which the total estimated time to completion from event 1 to event 15 is 47.5 weeks. Other paths—as may be shown by calculation—require less time; these are termed semicritical or slack paths, depending on how near they are to the critical path in terms of total time required. For example, path 1 — 3 — 8 — 13 — 15 consumes 40.0 weeks estimated time and may be called semicritical. Path 1 — 2 — 4 — 9 — 14 — 15, by contrast, requires an estimated 21.5 weeks to complete and is called a slack path. By reallocating some of the resources from the slack to the critical and semicritical paths, it may be possible to reduce the overall project completion time and project costs.

The critical path method has other adaptations which are quite similar to PERT. In one such procedure, only two time estimates are used to characterize the activity linking successive events. The first is the *all normal* estimate (the same as the t_m estimate in PERT), and the second is the *all crash* estimate for the activity completion time when no cost is spared to reduce the time to a minimum.

CPM and PERT methods are best suited for project management rather than for continuous or ongoing management operations. Moreover, because of the relatively high implementation cost, they are best applied to large and complex projects. Small projects with a limited number of activities do not require the quantitative sophistication of CPM or PERT. One practical asset of these methods is that they permit *management by exception.* Management need pay little attention to activities that are on schedule; the technique identifies those activities that are not being accomplished within the time estimates; management by emergency is thus eliminated because emergencies are predicted and can be averted.

Both CPM and PERT easily lend themselves to periodic updating and revision as the project proceeds toward completion. In this sense they can be used as effective management control methods. However, they do not allow for the possibility that a network activity may not succeed or may not be needed.

Figure 4-5. A PERT network (time estimates shown in calendar weeks).

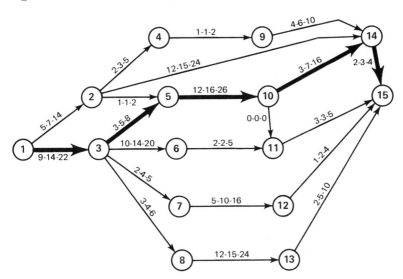

SOURCE: H.F. Evarts, *Introduction to PERT*. Boston: Allyn and Bacon, 1964. Used with permission.

Likewise, no provision is made for the possibility that major revisions internal to the program may be needed or that the entire project may have to be abandoned.[16]

REFERENCES

1. M. Meyerson, "Price of Admission into the Defense Business," *Harvard Business Review*, July/August 1967, pp. 111–123.
2. E. J. Kelley, *Marketing: Strategy and Functions*. Englewood Cliffs, N.J.: Prentice-Hall, Inc., 1965.
3. W. D. Zarecor, "High-Technology Product Planning," *Harvard Business Review*, March/April 1967, pp. 108–115.
4. B. F. Petrini and P. D. Grub, "Product Management in High Technology Defense Industry Marketing," *California Management Review*, Vol. 15, No. 3, 1973, pp. 138–146.
5. S. F. Divita, "Selling R&D to the Government," *Harvard Business Review*, September/October 1965, pp. 62–75.
6. P. O. Soelberg, *Industrial Management Review*, Spring 1967, pp. 19–29.

7. J. Bjorksten, "Bidding Strategy," address delivered before the National Conference on the Management of Aerospace Programs of the American Aeronautical Society, University of Missouri, November 16, 1966.
8. E. B. Roberts, "The Measurement and Improvement of R&D Marketing Effectiveness," Fifth Annual Management Conference on Marketing in the Defense Industries, May 10, 1968.
9. T. Bond and G. Brickman, *The Proposal Preparation Cycle*. San Diego: Paragon Design Co., 1967.
10. J. R. Bright, *A Brief Introduction to Technology Forecasting*. Austin, Texas: The Pemaquid Press, 1972.
11. D. W. Ewing (Ed.), "Top-Management Guides for Research Planning," in *Long Range Planning for Management*. New York: Harper and Row, Publishers, 1964, pp. 362–396.
12. R. U. Ayres, *Technological Forecasting and Long-Range Planning*. New York: McGraw-Hill Book Co., 1969.
13. J. P. Dory and R. J. Lord, "Does TF Really Work?" *Harvard Business Review*, November/December 1970, p. 16.
14. J. B. Quinn, "Technological Forecasting," *Harvard Business Review*, March/April 1967, p. 101.
15. H. F. Evarts, *Introduction to PERT*. Boston: Allyn and Bacon, Inc., 1964.
16. J. J. Moder and C. R. Phillips, *Project Management with CPM and PERT*. New York: Reinhold Publishing Corp., 1964.

LEGAL ASPECTS OF R&D MANAGEMENT 5

The shrike hunting the locust is unaware of the hawk hunting him.

This chapter deals with several topics of a legal nature which are of considerable importance to the R&D manager. The treatment is intended only to provide a basis for lay understanding of matters concerning the R&D procurement process, product and process protection, and liability. In seeking an acceptable balance between practical utility and precision of legal expression, some compromises are necessary. Therefore, prudence would indicate that counsel of experienced contracting officers or legal authorities be sought in matters of a particular nature touched upon here only in general terms.

PROCUREMENT

In Chapter 4 the concept of a product life cycle was described and was related to the notion of the life cycle of an advanced technological system. According to Department of Defense terminology, as such a system moves successfully forward in time it passes through six evolutionary stages:

Research
Exploratory development
Advanced development
Engineering development
Management support
Operational systems development

This R&D program cycle averages about eight years to completion for major systems development. Following cycle completion the system moves on to production, which typically spans some two to five years.

The Procurement Cycle

Tightly woven into the fabric of the R&D program cycle is the *procurement cycle,* which includes all activities associated with letting an R&D contract. Since a major systems development effort may require the execution and coordination of a great many subcontracts, such an R&D program cycle may be composed of many procurement cycles.

Procurement cycles differ radically in complexity. As an example of the cycle in its simplest form, a project engineer working for a commercial firm may decide that an outside contractor is required to support his program; following discussions and a brief proposal in the form of a letter from his designated contractor, a purchase order for services is written. This illustrates in bare minimum the streamlined procurement cycle as it moves through a sequence of stages: problem definition, selection of and consultation with a contractor, formal offer for contract services, and contract award. The time required to execute such a cycle may be as short as a week or a great deal longer, depending on the nature of the delays that may arise to impede procurement cycle progress.

Federal R&D procurement, however, is usually another matter. Each of the many departments and agencies of the federal government is required by law to follow rather rigid formal procedures throughout the procurement cycle. Figure 5-1 illustrates the sequence of events as they occur in a typical federal procurement cycle.[1] Deviations from the process can and do appear, as illustrated, although in the case of major DOD systems acquisitions deviations are minor. This procurement process is indeed formidable in its complexity and the entire cycle may take as much as a year or longer to complete. Such thoroughness is necessary, however, to permit as fair and objective a procurement of R&D services as can reasonably be made. The cost of the

Figure 5-1. Flow of formal activities in a typical research and development contract award. The boldface boxes, in most instances, apply only to large contracts (exceeding $1 million).

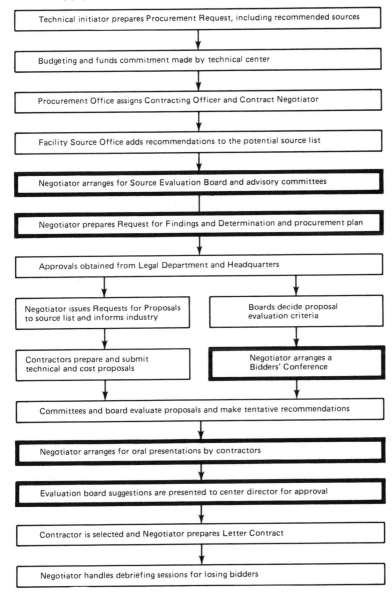

SOURCE: Adapted from D. Allison (Ed.), *The R&D Game: Technical Men, Technical Managers, and Research Productivity.* Cambridge, Mass.: M.I.T. Press, 1969. Used with permission.

process in consequence is high, not only in terms of the effort required of government and civil service personnel in carrying forth the process, but also in terms of the contractors' proposal response efforts, part or all of the cost of which is passed on to the government through overhead.

It is important to recognize that the federal government exercises considerable authority over contractors' costs. It has the right to audit the costs not only of particular federal contracts but, in many cases, of the contractor's entire operations. It is not unusual to find federal auditors in on-site residence in high-technology R&D organizations; their business is to examine and audit costs, with the authority to allow or disallow certain contract costs.

In most federal procurements, multiple-source solicitations are sought from all interested and qualified contractors. In recent times, however, this open-door policy has been labeled as inequitable to smaller, more specialized commercial firms whose federal markets are restricted by the overpowering competition of the large, broadly based R&D organizations. In an effort to support the small R&D manufacturing or consulting firm, many federal procurements today exclude larger organizations from competing in bidding programs that are the "proper domain" of the small business. The dimensions of a *small business concern* are defined by the Small Business Administration. The term applies to a concern that is independently owned and operated, is not dominant in the field of operation in which it is bidding on government contracts, and succeeds in meeting the SBA criteria for size in relation to the industry involved.

Commercial organizations are of course generally free of outside restrictions on their procurement processes. They enjoy much greater latitude in deciding whether or not multiple-source solicitations are to be sought, or whether a sole-source contract is in its own best interests. This flexibility is valuable, for the firm can be more pragmatic in determining the optimum *cost to procure* and can tailor procurement procedures to the value expected to be added through the selection method. Nevertheless, over the years most larger organizations have developed as a matter of general policy certain procurement procedures which resemble in many respects the federal procurement process. The remainder of this discussion on procurement illustrates and compares the basic features of federal and commercial procurement cycles.

Armed Services and Federal Procurement

Procurement of goods and services by contract with the federal government has a long evolutionary history.[2] The beginnings of the federal procurement process can be traced to the year 1792, when the Department of the Treasury was given full responsibility for making purchases and contracts for the Army. In 1809 the requirement that all procurements be formally advertised was placed on the purchase of all government supplies and services. This requirement was reaffirmed and refined through several federal acts throughout the nineteenth century. During the period 1937–1940, influenced by events foreshadowing World War II, major changes were wrought which signaled the transition from mandatory use of formal advertising to the complete use of negotiated contracts.

During the early 1940s new procedures were introduced to streamline the procurement process by emphasizing speed and by favoring contractors having full existing in-house capabilities. The experience gained in using negotiated contracts during this critical time of international conflict showed that they were feasible and had advantages in certain procurement situations. The next major milestone in the evolution of the federal procurement process took place in 1947 with the Armed Services Procurement Act, which for the first time provided for both formal advertising and negotiated contracts within the federal government. The Armed Services Procurement Act has been greatly expanded in the years since, but continues to serve as the cornerstone for today's federal procurement policy.

Before describing the shape of modern procurement policy it is important to draw the distinction between procurement by *formal advertising* and procurement by *negotiation*. Formal advertising is the basic procurement procedure used today in nearly all state and municipality purchases, and is the preferred mode within the federal government. Basically, the buyer solicits bids on the anticipated procurement from qualified bidders by advertising and issuing an IFB (Invitation for Bid) to all requestors. In the case of armed services and federal procurements the invitations are usually issued through the *Commerce Business Daily*, a publication of the Department of Commerce. The IFB contains all specifications a contractor needs to draw up his bid. When the bids are received, they are posted, opened in public, and reviewed to determine which bids meet all the stated requirements. The contract is then awarded to the responsive, responsible bidder whose bid is lowest, whose price is fair, and whose offering is judged to be most advantageous to the government.

Procurement by negotiation, on the other hand, involves soliciting proposals from prospective contractors by issuing an RFP (Request for Proposal) to interested requestors. Often, as in R&D projects whose technical requirements are not well established at the outset, the buyer may ask prospective contractors to furnish a preproposal, in which the contractor formulates the problem and his proposed solution so that the buyer can review them before the RFP is written and distributed. When the proposals are finally received in response to the RFP, the contractor offering the best combination of approach, experience, and proposed cost is selected, with final costs subject to negotiation. There are circumstances in which a contract may be awarded to a contractor on a *sole-source* basis, that is, noncompetitively, if it can be established that it is in the government's best interests to do so.

Formal advertising is used where the procurement goals as well as the technology are well established. It is singularly objective in approach. Procurement through negotiation, on the other hand, is used where the goals and/or the technology cannot be precisely stated, and leads to an evaluation process that is much more subjective in approach.

The federal contracting field today centers around the basic *Armed Services Procurement Regulation* (ASPR) for military buying and the *Federal Procurement Regulations* (FPR) for civilian agency buying. The ASPR document is the contracting authority for the Department of Defense, and the provisions of the

document serve as the basic authority for all military procurements. The FPR document covers the basic procurement policy
for all the federal civilian agencies, and is augmented and implemented by regulations issued by the various civilian agencies. The contents of both the ASPR and the FPR are contained
in a set of eight volumes, periodically revised, collectively entitled the *Government Contracts Reporter*[3] (a nongovernment
publication). Contained within these several thousand pages are
detailed policies and procedures for federal procurement, together with explanations furnishing an overall view of the official
requirements and including topically arranged digests of court
and administrative decisions to show how the rules have been
applied. The following procurement regulations are contained in
the *Government Contracts Reporter:*

Armed Services Procurement Regulation (ASPR)
Army Procurement Procedure (APP)
Defense Supply Procurement Regulations (DSPR)
Air Force ASPR Supplement
Energy Research and Development Administration Procure-
    ment Regulations (ERDA PR)
Navy Procurement Directives (NPD)
Federal Procurement Regulations (FPR)
General Services Administration Procurement Regulations
    (GSPR)
National Aeronautics and Space Administration Procurement
    Regulations (NASA PR)

In addition, procurement regulations issued by the Coast Guard,
the Corps of Engineers, and the Federal Aviation Agency are
described.

The ASPR and the FPR are the basic instruments used by
contracting officers of both parties to federal procurements. The
regulations are extensive, detailed, and frequently updated, and
the R&D manager will normally acquire at best only a casual
knowledge of them. The ASPR procedures set forth general policy for practically all procurement activities for which appropri-
ated funds are to be used. To derive full information on a procurement question it is therefore necessary to consult both the

ASPR and the particular department or agency supplement. At present the trend in government procurement circles is toward expanding the ASPR with the eventual goal of eliminating supplementary procedures.[2]

Program managers find themselves in frequent communication with contracting specialists in all phases of the R&D process, from proposal preparation through program execution and termination. Despite the technical complexity of federal procure-

Figure 5-2. Armed Services Procurement Regulation (ASPR) contents.

SECTION	TITLE
1.	GENERAL PROVISIONS
2.	PROCUREMENT BY FORMAL ADVERTISING
3.	PROCUREMENT BY NEGOTIATION
4.	SPECIAL TYPES AND METHODS OF PROCUREMENT
5.	INTERDEPARTMENTAL AND COORDINATED PROCUREMENT
6.	FOREIGN PURCHASES
7.	CONTRACT CLAUSES
8.	TERMINATION OF CONTRACTS
9.	PATENTS, DATA, AND COPYRIGHTS
10.	BONDS, INSURANCE, AND INDEMNIFICATION
11.	TAXES
12.	CONTRACTOR INDUSTRIAL LABOR RELATIONS
13.	GOVERNMENT PROPERTY
14.	PROCUREMENT QUALITY ASSURANCE
15.	CONTRACT COST PRINCIPLES AND PROCEDURES
16.	PROCUREMENT FORMS
17.	EXTRAORDINARY CONTRACTUAL ACTIONS
18.	CONSTRUCTION AND ARCHITECT-ENGINEER CONTRACTS
19.	TRANSPORTATION
20.	ADMINISTRATIVE MATTERS
21.	PROCUREMENT MANAGEMENT REPORTING SYSTEM
22.	SERVICE CONTRACTS
23.	SUBCONTRACTING POLICIES AND PROCEDURES
24.	PERSONAL PROPERTY IN POSSESSION OF CONTRACTOR
25.	PRODUCTION SURVEILLANCE AND REPORTING
26.	CONTRACT MODIFICATIONS

*Figure 5-3. Federal Procurement Regulations (FPR)
contents.*

PART	TITLE
1.	GENERAL
2.	PROCUREMENT BY FORMAL ADVERTISING
3.	PROCUREMENT BY NEGOTIATION
4.	SPECIAL TYPES AND METHODS OF PROCUREMENT
5.	SPECIAL AND DIRECTED SOURCES OF SUPPLY
6.	FOREIGN PURCHASES
7.	CONTRACT CLAUSES
8.	TERMINATION OF CONTRACTS
9.	PATENTS, DATA, AND COPYRIGHTS
10.	BONDS AND INSURANCE
11.	FEDERAL, STATE, AND LOCAL TAXES
12.	LABOR
14.	INSPECTION AND ACCEPTANCE
15.	CONTRACT COST PRINCIPLES AND PROCEDURES
16.	PROCUREMENT FORMS
17.	EXTRAORDINARY CONTRACTUAL ACTIONS TO FACILITATE THE NATIONAL DEFENSE
18.	PROCUREMENT OF CONSTRUCTION
19.	TRANSPORTATION
20.	RETENTION REQUIREMENTS FOR CONTRACTOR AND SUBCONTRACTOR RECORDS
26.	CONTRACT MODIFICATIONS
30.	CONTRACT FINANCING

ment regulations, R&D managers will find it useful to have a basic understanding of what is contained in the ASPR and FPR documents.

Figures 5-2 and 5-3 list the contents of the two documents by section. As can be seen by comparison, the contents of the ASPR and the FPR are nearly the same, and parallel each other quite closely through the first 19 parts (with the exception of ASPR Section 13, Government Property, which has no counterpart in the FPR).

While the ASPR sets forth regulations and procedures applicable to all military procurements, each branch of the Department of Defense has its own regulations to supplement the ASPR. The departments of the Army, Navy, and Air Force, as well as the National Aeronautics and Space Administration, all supplement the ASPR to implement and promulgate their own policies and procedures, especially where procurement circumstances arise which are not covered by the ASPR. In addition, the Energy Research and Development Administration (ERDA) issues its supplementary regulations to implement the FPR, as ERDA is part of the FPR system. ERDA procurement regulations are founded on those promulgated by its forerunner agency, the Atomic Energy Commission (AEC).

Commercial Procurement of R&D

Commercial procurement is distinguished from federal procurement principally in terms of its generally being much more streamlined. Commercial organizations are of course free of the encumberances of Armed Services and federal procurement regulations and are not bound to follow them.* On the other hand, many of the larger corporate enterprises which frequently purchase R&D services have developed procurement practices patterned after federal procurement procedures.

Since procurement practices among commercial organizations vary so greatly, it is not possible to discuss them within a consistent framework as can be done for government procurement practices. However, there are several useful guidelines which can serve the technical project engineer or manager in dealing with commercial procurements.

In the first place, the commercial buyer is usually not bound by law to advertise his intended procurement. He can, and frequently does, deal directly with his favored contractor in the purchase of R&D services. This saves both the buyer and the contractor valuable time as compared with the lengthy federal procurement cycle. Moreover, this direct practice is facilitated by the nature of the typical commercial R&D procurement; it is aimed at satisfying immediate needs quickly in situations where the problem and the technology are clearly known to both partners of the contract.

---

* There are of course various federal regulations to which commercial organizations are bound in doing business under contract, such as those pertaining to equal opportunity, for example.

Only rarely do commercial organizations contract with outside firms for long-range R&D needs. The R&D project life cycle is short relative to the growth of the organization, and the commercial firm must protect itself in the marketplace by capitalizing on its R&D program to develop innovative products and markets. Any R&D procured from outside contractors must therefore be of near-term interest designed to support new product development.

Furthermore, there are some differences between federal and commercial procurement in the negotiation phase. The commercial buyer is not in a legal position to require an audit of the contractor's records and proposed costs unless such an audit is provided for by contract. The cost basis is generally accepted on the strength of the contractor's reputation, although the total proposed contract cost, of course, is subject to modification to fit the customer's budget. Generally, contract negotiation is less important in the case of commercial procurements.

As in the case of federal procurement offices, the commercial organization has its favored types of contracts. In particular, most such organizations prefer a fixed-price contract format, for it ensures the procurement outcome (minimizes risk) and fits well into the corporate budget structure. Some organizations frequently buy R&D services with time-and-materials (T&M) contracts, although most view these as a form of fixed-price contract in that the work is expected to be completed within the original cost estimate.* On the other hand, because of the flexibility commercial organizations enjoy in the procurement cycle, cost and time overruns can often be accommodated much more easily than in the case of federal contracts.

Finally, one finds reporting and coordination functions to be generally more streamlined in the commercial contract. Frequently, these functions are conducted with a high degree of informality, by notes, telephone calls, and the like. Such informality, however, can breed problems for the project manager who fulfills his contract too casually, for misunderstandings can

---

* The fixed-price and time-and-materials contracts are described in the next section.

arise more easily when reporting and coordination functions are not clearly defined and understood.

R&D CONTRACTING

Contracts form the basis of nearly all research and development activities; it is therefore important that those responsible for R&D management understand the basic essentials of contracting. Contracts contain the provisions under which technical work is to be accomplished, as well as the regulations governing project management. All contracts differ from one another both in substance and in detail. Because contracts are legally binding instruments, technical personnel should never hesitate to consult with their cognizant contracting or legal officer for clarification and interpretation of contractual matters.

Armed with a basic understanding of contracts, the R&D manager can avoid many problems. (This section provides a brief description of the most common types of contracts found in R&D programs.) The R&D manager should realize that most organizations sponsoring research and development have their own favored types of contracts which they normally write. Organizational policy indicates which can and cannot be written, and therefore most procurement officers are unwilling to consider all the types of contracts discussed in this section. The reader is referred to Chapter 4 for related topics of proposal content and evaluation criteria (see sections "R&D Proposals—Preparation" and "R&D Proposals—Evaluation Criteria").

Research and development contracts are written to cover all possibilities across the whole spectrum of procurements, ranging from basic research through systems development, acquisition, and maintenance. Each has its special contract requirements. Basic research and exploratory development programs are characterized by lack of specific requirements and approaches, work that is difficult to plan in detail ahead of time, and lack of objective criteria by which to judge performance. Although usually associated with federal procurements, basic research and exploratory development are carried out in the private corporate sector by many of the larger high-technology organizations.[1] (See the section titled "Scope of R&D in the United States" in Chapter 1.)

In the center of the spectrum is the advanced development area of R&D, which is associated with procurement in instances where a given concept needs to be verified experimentally and demonstrated to be technically and logistically sound. It is in this area of R&D that significant hardware may be developed and tested, and more definite requirements and criteria for measuring technical performance can therefore be set forth.

The final stage of R&D concerns engineering and systems prototype development and production. It encompasses design concepts directed at meeting technical and cost objectives, and may involve prototype production to demonstrate all hardware and processes involved in production. Because the objectives are tightly specified, the goals and risks are usually quite clear to both parties to the contract.

Each of these phases of the R&D process requires contract types especially tailored to its own needs. Before describing some of the most common types of R&D contracts, however, a few basic concepts common to all contracts should be fixed.

To begin with, a contract is generally considered to be a legally binding and mutually acceptable agreement that includes an exchange of consideration or value. Each party should stand to gain something of value. A *valid contract* is therefore one whose terms are in full force and are enforceable by court action. In contrast, an *unenforceable contract* is one that would appear to be valid in all respects except that it is not enforceable through court action. For example, most states and the federal government are historically protected from being sued except by their own consent. Therefore, a contract with such a government entity may seem valid, but if permission to sue has not been specifically granted it is unenforceable except through the Court of Claims. Some contracts are written so that under specified conditions they may not be binding on one party. Such a contract is called a *voidable contract,* meaning that it is binding on one party but may or may not bind the second party at his option.

The concept of risk is also central to the mutual acceptance of a contract. Whereas value is mutually exchanged, risk may be assumed by one or both parties, and may be present in a degree from negligible to great. Risk is in turn related to the profit available to the contractor; the greater the risk, the more profit potential the contractor will insist upon. It is this balance between risk and reward that serves as the basis for the type of contract to be written in a given situation.

A number of factors come into play in the selection of type of contract. Among the more prominent are:

—The degree of confidence in the proposed price.
—The nature of the supplies or services being procured.
—The timing of the procurement: Is it a crash program?
—How important is the contract deadline to the buyer?
—Industry and organizational practices. Some procurement agencies forbid sole-source procurements, while others shun cost-type contracts.
—Degree of competition involved.
—Past performance of contractor.

With rare exceptions, it is the buyer who selects the type of contract to be written.

The contractor is responsible for fulfilling his obligations under a contract or else must be prepared to defend himself against claims by the commercial or government sponsor. For example, under certain circumstances the government may recover monetary damages from contractors for excess costs incurred in completing contract performance after default by the contractor, for actual damages as a result of the contractor's delay, for liquidated damages, for consequential damages, for damages from latent defects after acceptance, or for damages resulting from breach of an express contract warranty.

Most contracts fall into one of two broad categories: cost reimbursement and fixed price. Specific contract types belonging to these categories, as well as some which conform to neither, are described below.

Cost Reimbursement Contracts

Cost reimbursement contracts are used rather widely in federal procurements, especially in small- to moderate-size basic and exploratory research where specific R&D objectives are difficult to define. Under this category of contracts, the contractor pledges to do his best only in pursuing the broad objectives specified by the sponsoring agency, up to the limit of the contract funds. Beyond this there are no guarantees of results—other than for stated reporting requirements, of course. In return for his efforts, the contractor is reimbursed for reasonable and allowable costs* incurred up to a specified limit. In addition to reimbursement for costs, he may receive a fee or profit, usually allocated as a fixed percentage of the contractor's cost.

In all but unusual situations, the cost reimbursement type of procurement means that the contractor will spend the full contract amount and thereby earn his full fee. Exceptions may occur when the contract is terminated early, either because of lack of funds budgeted or because the technical goals proved to be unachievable for reasons previously unforeseen. Except for these extraordinary circumstances, however, the contractor will derive the full fee stated in the contract, and without assumption of risk. Thus there is no direct financial incentive on the part of the contractor for good cost management; rather, his incentive lies in maintaining or enhancing his reputation for technical performance.

Because of the weak incentive involved in cost reimbursement contracts, government contracting agencies are reluctant to engage in them except when required by the nature of the procurement. When this type of contract is indicated, the sponsoring organization will normally contract with a firm in which it has a high level of confidence based on past experience. It should be mentioned regarding incentive for cost control that federal policy specifically prohibits cost-plus-a-percentage-of-cost contracts or subcontracts. Such procurements would give contractors a negative incentive for cost control and would foster greater inefficiency.

Of the several types of cost reimbursement contracts normally used, perhaps the most common is the *cost-plus-fixed-fee* (CPFF) contract. Here the contractor is reimbursed for his best-efforts performance for reasonable and allowable costs incurred and is

---

* Certain expenditures for equipment, travel, subcontracting, and so forth, may be limited or disallowed altogether in the contract.

given a fee or profit, computed as a percentage of cost. The CPFF contract is used primarily for research studies and other limited R&D requirements where objectives can be stated only in rather broad terms. Closely related to the CPFF contract is the *cost-without-fee* contract. The only difference between the two is that in the latter, no fee is paid. It is otherwise applied in the same situations as the CPFF contract, but is used in connection with educational and nonprofit R&D foundations, as well as "captive" facilities wholly owned and funded by the government.

Various types of cost reimbursement contracts have been used in an effort to overcome the primary drawback of the CPFF contract, namely, the lack of incentive for control of contractor costs. One of these is the *cost-plus-award-fee* (CPAF) contract. Here the contractor's fee is composed of two parts: a fixed amount (based on a percentage—usually 3 percent—of cost) plus an amount (not to exceed 12 percent of contract cost) based on the buyer's subjective evaluation of the quality of performance as compared with contract specifications. The degree of incentive is adjusted by the relative weight given to these two components. Although the CPAF contract succeeds in providing some measure of cost control incentive, difficulties can arise unless contract specifications are specific enough that the quality of performance can be evaluated fairly to both parties' satisfaction. Thus, the CPAF contract has drawbacks when used for basic or exploratory research studies with loosely defined goals (the very kind of contractual situations for which cost reimbursement contracts are designed).

The *cost-plus-incentive-fee* (CPIF) contract provides another means of building in cost control incentives. In this contract the government pays for costs incurred up to the contract limit, and the fee is computed from a formula which compares the contractor's final cost to his estimated cost. The fee can result in a profit to the contractor if his costs are controlled so as not to exceed his estimates, or a loss to him if his costs are too excessive. Like the other CPAF contract, this method of fee allocation is appropriate only if the R&D goals and approaches for goal attainment are set forth with sufficient clarity to enable a meaningful assessment of performance.

Another type of cost reimbursement contract that is sometimes used in R&D is the *cost-sharing* contract. Cost sharing, or buying in, indicates the contractor's offer to receive no fee and to assume some portion of the costs he expects to incur in conducting the program; that is, he agrees to perform the required R&D at a net loss. A contractor might offer a cost-sharing arrangement if he believes this will buy his first R&D contract in an area that will open up new horizons to him in the future. The cost-sharing contract is used when the contractor in question is not among the leaders in a particular technology, and he finds competition otherwise too strong in that area to be competitive. Cost sharing is also used as a loss leader that will help guarantee award of a contract for a system design, with the broader objective of winning a lucrative follow-on production contract.

The practice of cost-sharing contracts is controlled by the ASPR, which generally discourages its use on grounds that its long-term effects may diminish competition and/or result in poor contract performance. Where there is reason to believe that buying in has occurred, contracting officers must give assurance that costs excluded from an initial contract are not recovered in follow-on contract work. The ASPR also prohibits contract award to a bidder if the sole reason for his being selected is his willingness to share costs. Cost sharing, however, is sometimes specifically required of the contractor, especially in cases where the contract effort is in the mutual interest of the government and the contractor (as in a government-owned, contractor-operated R&D facility). The ASPR places limits on cost participation in these cases.

Fixed-Price Contracts

As compared with cost reimbursement contracts, fixed-price contracts shift the burden of risk over to the contractor. It is for this reason that both federal and commercial R&D procurement agencies prefer a fixed-price contract whenever appropriate, even though it may mean somewhat higher R&D costs associated with higher contractor risk. In contrast to cost reimbursement contracts, a fixed-price contract *guarantees* contract performance, regardless of whether or not the contractor makes a profit. This guarantee not only provides the buyer with protection against risk but simplifies his budget process.

Under the provisions of a fixed-price contract the buyer pays a set price in return for the contractor's guarantee of performance. In contrast to the cost reimbursement type of contract, where the fee is set a priori, the contractor's fee under a fixed-price contract is directly related to his efficiency and ability to control costs. His profit is simply the difference between the contract cost and his incurred cost, and this profit can range from handsome to dismally nonexistent, depending on performance.

Certainly the most common type of fixed-price contract is the *firm-fixed-price* (FFP) contract, which is basically as described above: the contractor assumes all risks and is paid a set price in return for his assured performance. The FFP contract is applicable when the work scope and objectives are clearly stated, and sufficient historical cost data are available on which to base the cost estimate. It is used, for example, in military production contracts where specific design specifications are available and in commercial procurements where the specifications are clear and the technology is well established. In preparing his cost estimate for a fixed-price proposal, the contractor will estimate his costs and then add on a projected fee derived from his assessment of the risk in fulfilling contract obligations, his confidence in projected cost rates, his evaluation of the competition, and other factors.

Several variants of the FFP contract are available for use when uncertainties exist regarding costs or it is desired to reward superior contract performance. One of these is the *fixed-price-with-escalation* contract, which provides for uncontrollable fluctuations in materials or labor *rates* during contract performance. Upper and lower limits on costs are provided for in the contract for control purposes, and escalations (up or down) of materials and labor rates are provided for to cover uncertainties in raw materials and wage rates. This type of contract has application when there is doubt as to the stability of the supply market and labor conditions (as in anticipated union contract negotiations) through the duration of extended production periods. Note that this contract does not protect the contractor against poor estimates of materials or labor quantity. Fixed-price-with-escalation contracts are not often used because of the difficulty and cost involved in administering them.

The *fixed-price-incentive* contract is used where superior cost or time performance is desired, and technical and cost uncertainties can be reasonably identified. A profit formula is set forth in the contract, and the final profit is computed by this formula based on a comparison of estimated and actual cost and/or time performance. The contractor stands to gain or lose in accordance with this performance (as in the case of the CPIF contract); in either case he is legally obligated to fulfill the terms of the contract. There are limits to the application of this type of contract. It is most suitable for procurements in cases where some cost responsibility is desired of the contractor, where the contractor's accounting system can provide for cost revisions, and where the nature of the supplies or services discourages an FFP contract.

In procurement situations involving protracted periods of performance, the *prospective-price-redetermination* contract is designed to enable contract costs to be redetermined at stated intervals (usually 12 months or longer). Up until the time for price redetermination, the contract is a firm-fixed-price contract. In effect, this type of contract provides for a sequence of FFP contract segments, and is appropriate where fixed prices can be established for an initial phase but not for subsequent phases. An example would be a contract for the design, prototype development, and production of a military system.

Another special category of fixed-price procurement is the *retroactive-price-redeterminable-after-completion* contract. This contract establishes a ceiling price and retroactive price redetermination after project completion. During this final negotiation, provision is made for a profit margin through consideration of management effectiveness and the ingenuity exhibited by the contractor throughout the performance period. The weakness of this contract lies in the fact that it offers no objective incentive for cost control. It is usually used in circumstances where a reasonable price cannot be established at the time of initial negotiation and where the cost is so small and the performance period so short that other types of contracts are impractical.

There are many instances in basic and exploratory R&D where a fixed-price procurement is desired for work of a study nature. The *fixed-price–level-of-effort* contract provides for a firm fixed price for a specified level of effort over a stated period of time. Here the contractor is paid for his "best efforts" rather than for results achieved; therefore, as in the case of the CPFF contract, there is little incentive for effective cost control. This type of contract is especially suited for R&D efforts whose end results cannot be clearly defined and may even be unknown.

Other Kinds of Contracts

There are some contractual situations which are suited neither to cost reimbursement nor to fixed-price agreements. One of these is the *basic ordering agreement*, sometimes called a *task-type* contract. This contract is used when a buyer wishes to have a certain contractor available on a quick response basis over a period of time to perform various tasks that cannot be specifically foreseen. The contractor acts, in effect, as a consultant to his client. The contract is written to permit authorization of specific tasks, when needed, by letter, thereby avoiding the time-consuming formal procurement process each time. The basic ordering agreement contains price and time limits, and usually specifies the broad technical area under which the tasks are to fall.

Another commonly used contract is the *time-and-materials* (T&M) contract. This contract is a hybrid in that it is neither a cost reimbursement nor a fixed-price contract, yet has elements of both. It provides for costs (including fees) of labor rates and materials used for work of a continuing or repetitive nature over a specified length of time. Because the total quantity of work is unknown it is not a fixed-price contract, yet because the labor (and sometimes the materials) rates are fixed it is not a cost reimbursement contract either. It is used frequently for equipment repair, overhaul, maintenance, and similar work, and also for certain types of R&D where flexibility in work scope is desired. There is little direct incentive for efficiency since all costs are covered on any given job; for that reason the T&M contract is often used only where no other contract type is applicable. To protect the buyer against runaway costs, a ceiling cost is usually established, but this is subject to increase in the event that the quantity of work to be done exceeds initial estimates.

PRODUCT AND PROCESS PROTECTION

Patents

From the earliest times governments have attempted to stimulate creativity and inventiveness by granting patents and making inventions visible to the public to induce further inventiveness. The patent right is believed to have originated in Venice before the fifteenth century. The United States has issued patent rights from the very beginning. Massachusetts made patent rights part of its law even before the Revolution, and this right was later included in the U.S. Constitution in Article 1, Section 8, which reads in part:

> The Congress shall have power To promote the Progress of Science and useful Arts, by securing for limited times to Authors and Inventors the exclusive Right to their respective Writings and Discoveries.

In due course Congress exercised this power and the first U.S. Patent Act became law on April 10, 1790.

A patent is a grant of specified rights to an individual, individuals, or an organization by the government of a particular nation.* These rights generally consist of the exclusive right, for a limited time, to manufacture, use, and sell the patented invention and to exclude others from so doing. In a unanimous Supreme Court opinion of 1942, in the case of *Ethyl Gasoline Corporation et al. v. the United States,* the U.S. patent law was defined as that which "confers on the patentee a limited monopoly, the right or power to exclude all others from manufacturing, using, or selling his invention. The extent of that right is limited by the identification of his invention, as its boundaries are marked by the specifications and claims of the patent. He

---

* In the United States a patent may issue only to an individual or individuals; in some foreign countries a patent may also issue to a company.

may grant licenses to make, use, or vend, restricted in point of space or time, or with any other restriction upon the exercise of the granted privilege, save only that by attaching a condition to his license he may not enlarge his monopoly. . . . " This opinion has since been followed in many other court cases.

The primary purpose of the patent system is the advancement of the arts and sciences. The function of a patent is to add to the sum of useful knowledge, and one of the objectives of the patent system is to encourage dissemination of information concerning discoveries and inventions. The subject matter for which patents may be obtained covers practically every invention of an industrial character. In the United States, 35 United States Code 101 provides that "whoever invents or discovers any new and useful process, machine, manufacture, or composition of matter or any new and useful improvement thereof, may obtain a patent therefor, subject to the conditions and requirements of this title." In addition, the Code provides for design and plant patents. Among other things, patents are not granted for scientific principles or their new application through purely intellectual processes. For example, patents are not granted for computer software packages.

The patentability of an invention depends on three essential criteria: (1) newness or novelty, (2) usefulness or utility, and (3) nonobviousness. Of these criteria the last is the most subjective. In 35 United States Code 103 there is a provision that a patent may *not* be obtained "if the differences between the subject matter sought to be patented and the prior art are such that the subject matter as a whole would have been obvious at the time the invention was made to a person having ordinary skill in the art to which said subject matter pertains." It is intended to deny patent protection to trivial modifications of existing products or processes.

The United States is one of several nations which have adopted a preexamination procedure for evaluating patentability. Under this system, in advance of formal filing, an attempt is made to determine whether the application meets the requirements for a patent. This screening process is usually accomplished by a patent attorney or agent who, for a fee, searches relevant prior patents to evaluate the apparent newness, utility, and nonobviousness of the invention when compared with the prior art. At the conclusion of his search the attorney or agent reports his findings to his client, the inventor, with his assessment as to whether the product or process may be patentable in whole or in part. With this information the inventor must then decide if he wishes to pursue a patent or to abandon further action.

After the preexamination procedure has been completed and a decision has been made to apply for a patent, the patent application is prepared by the patent attorney or patent agent. The application must meet rigid federal standards pertaining to such matters as disclosure, description, drawings, and examples of the invention in language sufficiently clear that a person knowledgeable in the area could make and use the invention. The application must specify the characteristics of the invention which set it apart from prior patents already issued, and the claims must specifically cover the invention. The skill used in setting forth the claims often determines whether or not a patent will issue and also plays an important role in the patent's future commercial value.

When the patent application is filed it is assigned a serial number which it carries throughout the period of prosecution. The filing date and serial number, along with the patent application and all other information submitted or received by the Patent Office during the prosecution of the patent, are considered confidential information. None of this information will be released to any third party by the Patent Office without the proper authorization from the inventor or his attorney. The backlog of patent applications in the Patent Office usually causes a delay of approximately one year after the application is filed before any action is taken on the case by a patent examiner.

After the first action has been taken by the patent examiner the elapsed time before a patent will issue (if one does eventually issue) can vary substantially depending on the decision of the examiner as to the patentability of the claims. Sometimes the delay between the filing date and the final issuing or rejection of a patent can be as much as two to three years. If the claims are rejected even after being amended and defended by the patent attorney, an appeal can be filed in the Patent Office. Further appeals can carry the case up through the U.S. Supreme Court.

If a patent issues, it will be assigned a patent number and the abstract will be published in the U.S. Patent Office *Official Gazette.* Copies of the patent are available to anyone and can be ordered from the U.S. Patent Office at 50 cents per copy. In addition, after the patent has issued, all the information in the file becomes public information and is available to any third party on payment of appropriate costs and fees.

In the United States a patent is granted for a term of 17 years from the date it issues and will be granted only to the inventor or inventors. In many countries (but not in the United States) a periodic payment of fees is required subsequent to the filing of a patent to maintain the patent in force. This system is intended to ensure that patents in which the owner is no longer interested will be dropped from consideration as a subsisting monopoly, and also to avoid compulsory licensing.

The infringement of a patent consists in the unauthorized exercise of any rights granted to the inventor, such as unauthorized manufacture, use, or sale. When his exclusive rights have been infringed, the inventor may file suit in court to recover damages as well as to obtain an injunction prohibiting future infringement. In deciding an infringement suit, the court may not only adjudicate the infringement question but may also reconsider the validity of the patent itself.

The problems and policies surrounding the ownership and use of patents, the liabilities for their infringement, the licensing of patent rights, and the related problem of royalties present a complex and changing area of civil law. Federal statutes dealing with patent problems are relatively few and are directed at particular problem areas rather than at the subject as a whole. Administrative regulations are contained in Section 9 of both the ASPR and the FPR, and in the parallel sections of other agency regulations.

In general, federal policy with respect to the ownership of patent rights to inventions and discoveries made in the course of performance of government contract work varies from agency to agency.* There are many basic conflicting questions: Are the inventions thus developed best exploited in government possession or in the hands of the inventor? Does contractor ownership of a patent developed at government expense give an unfair advantage to the contractor and act against the public good? Will a contractor put forth his best efforts under contracts which vest the government with title to patents developed in the performance of contract R&D? And similar questions.

Federal policy generally intends to protect the public interest by granting the government title to inventions wherein the nature of the work or the government's past investments in the field favors full public access to resulting inventions. Within this policy, however, is the recognition that the public is better served by giving exclusive patent rights to a contractor in cases where it is likely that the contractor with exclusive rights will develop the technology further than would otherwise happen if the invention becomes freely available to all.

Some agencies, such as NASA and ERDA, have a policy which provides that the government will receive all right and title to and interest in all inventions conceived or first actually reduced to practice in the course of or under a government contract. The Department of Defense, however, generally follows a comprehensive license policy, under which the contractor retains all right and title to and interest in all inventions, but must grant to the government an irrevocable, nonexclusive, and royalty-free license to practice and have practiced the patent for government purposes throughout the world.

A *background patent* is a U.S. or foreign patent covering an invention which was not conceived or reduced to practice in the course of a government contract, and which is owned or con-

---

* The federal government usually claims unlimited rights to data when such data are developed during performance of R&D under a contract sponsored by the government.

trolled by an organization that has the right to license others. It is a patent which cannot be reasonably avoided during the use of any specific process, method, machine, manufacture, or composition of matter which is a subject of a proposed or current contract or subcontract for R&D technology.

United States common law holds that when an invention is made by an employee utilizing the facilities of his employer and/or in relation to the work he is performing for his employer, the employer acquires a right to such invention. However, an organization does not normally wish to acquire rights to inventions made by its employees if such inventions do not relate in some direct way to organizational interests or markets, or do not relate to the work being performed by the employee for the employer. Most companies have specific clauses in their employment contracts by which the employee agrees to assign to his employer all his right and title to and interest in any invention he conceives during the course of his employment, provided such invention relates to the work he is performing for his employer. This arrangement is necessary since in the United States a patent will be granted only to the inventor or inventors. Consequently, the use of an appropriate assignment provides for the transfer of all right, title, and interest to the employer.

Most large organizations engaged in R&D do provide some kind of reward or recognition for employee inventions. The rewards range from small lump-sum cash awards to a percentage of the royalties received from the licensing of the patent. Other organizations consider an employee's patents in evaluating his overall performance for salary increase or promotion.

In the case of the federal government, policy vests in the government entire right and title to and interest in all inventions made and developed by any government employee during working hours, with government equipment, funds, or information, and which bear a direct relation to the inventor's prescribed duties. If, however, the government's interest in the invention is insufficient to warrant its ownership of the patent, the agency concerned may release to the inventor all right and title to and interest in the invention subject to a reservation by the government of an irrevocable nonexclusive and royalty-free license to practice and have practiced the invention for government purposes throughout the world.

Licensing

In many cases an organization that owns all right and title to and interest in a patent as a result of an assignment or a purchase agreement may not be in a position to capitalize on the patent and derive the fullest potential benefit from it. The organization may not be in a position to manufacture and sell the invention because of limited manufacturing or marketing capabilities, or because the invention may not be compatible with existing product lines. If this is the case, several options may be available to the organization to realize profit potential from the invention. Two of these are:

—Manufacture the invention, and license other organizations to market it.

—License other organizations to manufacture, use, and market the invention.

Either of these courses may be chosen with the hope of realizing immediate gain, depending on the licensee's manufacturing and marketing capabilities.

Occasionally, a new product or process that has been patented may have a future value that is more attractive to the company than its current value. In this case the patent may be held to protect the product or process from competition while the investment in production facilities is amortized or until the time arrives when the product is more marketable.[5]

If an organization holds a patent on an invention and decides to manufacture and/or market it through a licensing agreement or series of agreements, it will recover part of the profit potential in *royalties*. These are cash returns resulting from authorizing an outside organization, by license, to manufacture, use, and sell the patented product. The license agreement is a contract giving limited or unrestricted, exclusive or nonexclusive right, for a stated period of time, to an outside firm to manufacture or market an invention. Usually, the license is granted in exchange for royalty payments, although there may be other considerations.*

Terms and conditions of various kinds may be included in the license agreement, provided they do not violate statutes such as antitrust laws. For example, a *tying clause* whereby the licensee is required to purchase materials and supplies from the patent holder would, in most cases, be held illegal. Royalties derived from licensing patented technology can be an important income source for companies having an investment in R&D but having limited production or marketing capabilities.

Often confusion arises over the meaning of the terms patent, copyright, and trademark. A *copyright* is a right granted by the federal government to an author, composer, artist, and so forth, whereby he may control his work or realize benefit from it. The copyright is designed to stimulate the creation and dissemination of creative work by providing recognition and reward to the author. Present U.S. code defines a copyright as "original works of authorship fixed in any tangible medium of expression, now known or later developed, from which they can be perceived, reproduced, or otherwise communicated, either directly or with the aid of a machine or device." Protection extends to written, pictorial, audio, and theatrical works, but not to ideas, processes, principles, and the like. The owner of a copyright has exclusive rights to do (or authorize to do) reproduction, preparation of derivative works, or distribution of the copyrighted work for sale, lease, rental, or transfer of ownership.

Whereas a patent can be granted only after meeting the criteria of novelty, utility, and inventiveness, a copyright can be granted for any original and expressive work as long as it was done independently—whether or not similar works exist. Even though the criteria for granting a copyright are less stringent than for granting a patent, a copyright enjoys substantial protection and is in force for the author's entire life and fifty years thereafter. Like

* Under the Military Assistance Program and for other national defense purposes, the government has an interest in developing foreign sources of supply. This is done through agreement called *foreign licensing* or *technical assistance* agreements, under which a domestic concern (primary source) agrees to furnish to a foreign concern or government (second source) patent rights and technical assistance.

a patent, a copyright is a monopoly, but is somewhat more limited by law. As with patent law, copyright law is constantly
changing and the general law in this field varies considerably
from country to country.

A *trademark* is a distinctive mark used to distinguish the
products of one producer from those of other producers. As defined in Section 45 of the Trademark Act of 1946, a trademark
"includes any word, name, symbol, or device, or any combination thereof adopted and used by a manufacturer or merchant to
identify his goods and distinguish them from those manufactured
or sold by others." Its basic function is to identify the origin of
the product to which it is affixed. Herein lies the primary distinction between a patent and a trademark: the purpose of the patent
is not to indicate origin but to protect the investors' rights in a
new product or process, irrespective of origin.

As with patents and copyrights, trademarks enjoy legal protection. A trademark offers a monopoly of sorts, since it provides the
owner with the exclusive right to use the mark. Its value is derived from its function as a visual assurance of the source or
manufacture of the product bearing the mark, thereby both creating and maintaining a demand for the product. A *registered
mark,* or one for which application to register has been filed, may
be assigned or licensed with the goodwill of the organization.

Trade Secrets

Patents are the most common form of protection for new products or processes of technology. In addition, however, the device
known as the *trade secret* offers a legitimate and effective means
of market protection. A trade secret is simply a means used in the
business world for restricting information on formulas, designs,
systems, or compiled information, thus giving the entrepreneur
an opportunity to obtain an advantage over competitors who do
not know or use the secret. Courts have held that a bona fide
trade secret must involve information that exhibits "a quantum of
novelty and originality, [is] generally unpublished, and
provide[s] a 'competitive advantage' over competitors who do
not use it.[6]

Within recent years trade secrets have enjoyed a certain degree of protection by the courts, although interpretations of trade secret law vary widely. In general, such law recognizes the organization's right to protect proprietary information from competitors. In view of recent U.S. Supreme Court rulings on the subject, however, it appears that the courts are moving toward increased judicial preemption of trade secret rights. In 1969 Mr. Justice Hugo Black declared in a dissenting opinion* that trade secrets do not exist in law unless patented: "no state has a right to authorize any kind of monopoly on what is claimed to be a new invention except when a patent has been obtained from the Patent Office under the exacting standards of the patent laws."[6] Many times a trade secret does not qualify as an invention, and therefore would not be within the concept described by Mr. Justice Black.

Notwithstanding the legal aspects of trade secret law, trade secrets offer an attractive practical alternative to patents and copyrights as a means of protecting proprietary information. In many cases an organization would rather avoid the time, expense, and risk involved in the more common patent procedures; they choose therefore to enshroud the project with secrecy and capitalize on it immediately. After all, once a patent has issued the entire file accumulated during the prosecution of the patent becomes public information, making it easy for competitors to analyze and imitate the product or process, thereby weakening the advantages the patent is supposed to provide.

Thus the trade secret option in some cases provides the organization with a better advantage over its competition than other options provide, while at the same time it denies the competition the information it requires to compete effectively in the marketplace. There can be little doubt that the trade secret mechanism has led to much industrial spying, and this has stimulated much recent legal work on the problem. At the present time, trade secret theft can be considered a felonious civil or criminal offense, punishable by imprisonment.

Espionage technology has developed to the point that many executives are concerned about trade secret theft, while detec-

---

* *Lear, Inc. v. Adkins.* This opinion has since been followed by many lower courts.

tive agencies are enjoying a growing business in safeguarding
organizations from those who would steal proprietary technology. Despite efforts to protect such assets from outside forces,
most violations come from within the organization, as a result of
carelessness or opportunistic indescretion. Without doubt a
major consideration underlying trade secret theft is the strong
technological orientation of our society, which drives organizations to develop better products and processes. This heightening
competition has tempted some firms to copy patents and equipment designs rather than rely on the uncertainties of the innovative process. To combat this trend, some authorities have rec-
ommended formal, but indirect, monitoring of competing
technology by assessing new patent applications, research contracts, and resource commitments in various technical areas.

As brought out above, a trade secret generally is considered to
be a property right that is afforded protection under law from
fraudulent access by outside parties. However, it is quite legitimate to uncover a trade secret through the practice of *reverse
engineering*, that is, starting with a finished product or process
and working backward in logical fashion to discover the underlying new technology. This practice is common within the automotive industry, for example, where manufacturers regularly purchase and tear down their competitors' vehicles to keep abreast
of (and frequently adopt) the others' new technology.

Further aggravating the security of trade secrets in R&D organizations is the lessening commitment engineers and scientists have to their employer. The high mobility of such persons is
related not only to current societal patterns but also to industrial
instabilities caused by large contract awards. R&D technologists
are often parties to inside knowledge of inventions and other
proprietary information; such favored individuals are then lured
to a competing organization by the offer of higher salaries and
promotions.

Employers, for many years, have sought to control such leak-
age to rival organizations by requiring new employees to sign
nondisclosure or nonuse agreements as a condition of employment. Such *employment contracts* have the implicit threat of
legal action against the former employee and his new employer

should proprietary information be leaked; they therefore probably prevent the loss of some trade secrets. Nevertheless, the protection afforded by employee contracts is limited by court interpretation of the common law concepts of unfair competition regarding trade secrets.[6] Such contracts do not obligate the former employee to forgo exercise of his inventive talents even though they may be inspired by knowledge and experience gained during the performance of his former duties. His efficiency and skills developed through that experience are considered to belong to him and not to his former employer.

Authorities differ as to the degree and type of measures needed to protect trade secrets. Some emphasize personnel screening as important; others argue for legal or plant protection.[7] Most agree, however, that the need for protecting trade secrets has its basis in four primary areas:

The rising cost and difficulty of litigation
Changing legal interpretations in court decisions
Rising employee mobility
Decline in employee loyalty

Many organizations have come to recognize that gentlemen's agreements between firms engaged in common areas of R&D can be used to slow intraindustrial mobility. These agreements serve as norms or unofficial guidelines to discourage the practice of pirating another firm's employee or hiring one who applies for a position.

PRODUCT LIABILITY

Of mounting concern to producing industries and the public at large is liability incurred by both producers and consumers through the use or misuse of products. This aspect of civil law has recently undergone radical change,* and it is important that the R&D manager understand how these changes in product

* For practical purposes the Uniform Commercial Code, adopted by nearly every state, forms the basis for product liability and warranties. This Code deals with such matters as notice, obligations, and labeling, but does not address the question of negligence.

liability might affect his responsibilities. While much attention is paid to consumer products, product liability questions arise often in connection with materials, systems, and other products of advanced technology.

The history of manufacturers' product liability can be traced back some four thousand years, to the kingdom of Babylonia. There, craftsmen who were found guilty of producing substandard wares were punished. However, under the dictum of *caveat emptor* ("let the buyer beware"), the customer who was injured through purchase of the products was afforded no compensation. With the passage of centuries the concept of consumer protection emerged, and the notion of *caveat venditor* ("let the seller beware") began to appear in early English common law. Gradually, the law developed various types of implied *warranties*, that is, the responsibility the manufacturer assumes that his product is fit for the use intended merely because he is in that business. To remove the vagaries of the implied warranty, the express warranty (one that is stated orally or in writing) came into being. Today most express warranties are a combination of a warranty or promise of fitness and a *guarantee*, that is, a promise of refund for a defective product.

Product liability generally arises from a defective design, manufacture, instruction, label, service, installation, or application that should have been foreseen by the designer, manufacturer, or seller. To have a valid legal claim, the injured party must demonstrate that physical or mental injury, or property damage, resulted from such negligence or defective design.* Litigation involving product liability is increasing dramatically, as shown here:

Year	NUMBER OF CLAIMS (thousands)
1960	negligible
1968	100
1970	500
1973	700–1,000

---

* Negligence and defective design generally constitute separate legal approaches to recovery of damages.

This increase is due in part to the dollar value of the awards, which routinely are in six figures and occasionally twelve, and to the number and complexity of products and systems sold. In addition, concern for consumer protection has focused attention on product liability. Data published in 1973 by the Consumer Products Safety Commission report that an estimated 20 million Americans are injured annually by products used in and around the house; of these, 110,000 are permanently disabled and 30,000 are killed. The economic cost to the nation for these injuries has been estimated at $5.5 billion.

Courts presently are moving in the direction of holding a product defective in design if it is unfit for all uses *and abuses* that can reasonably be foreseen. In practice one frequently finds this attitude goes hand in hand with the so-called *deep-pockets theory* of tort liability: the party with the deepest pockets (i.e., the most money) carries the burden of liability. However, the current trend in law is to hold that all damages suffered by the consumer or user are the responsibility of the organization that placed the product into channels of commerce. That is, he who profits is responsible.

Many states have enacted legislation providing for *comparative negligence.* This doctrine compares the negligence of the parties when negligence alone is the basis for recovery and when death or physical injury to persons or properties is a consequence of the negligence. Further, any damages allowed are diminished in proportion to the amount of negligence attributable to the persons or party recovering the damages.

The best way to limit litigation related to product liability claims is by using design and manufacturing procedures which will result in fault-free products and services. While this ideal standard may not always be achievable, certain methods can be employed to approach the fault-free standard.

The first area to address in limiting product liability is that of product or systems design. The overriding design objective in terms of product liability should be to anticipate problems that might arise through reasonable use or misuse. Design should be based on accepted principles using verified performance data that can be recalled and supported at a future date. This places a responsibility on the designer not only to generate data using accepted procedures but also to document permanently any data that may have been acquired indirectly and that could be held to be of doubtful validity or applicability.

Strict adherence to standards is essential if the design is to meet minimum levels of acceptance. Standards exist in two forms: those that are generally accepted and those that are internally developed and applied. Generally accepted design standards include those that are promulgated by various technical organizations such as the American Society of Mechanical Engineers (ASME), the American Society of Testing and Materials (ASTM), and the Society of Automotive Engineers (SAE), and standards that are imposed by federal agencies such as the Nuclear Regulatory Commission. In addition to these, nearly all organizations involved in the design of products that use new technology develop and impose on themselves certain standards of design. This is particularly true when accepted design standards do not exist and the designer feels it is important to adhere to some rational standards.

Protection against product liability is also afforded in the final design stages by submitting the design prototype to an independent testing laboratory for unbiased evaluation. Such action lends credibility to design claims and increases confidence in the design by exposing it to the critical eyes of unbiased experts who were not involved in the design process.

In addition to the design area, product liability is also affected by the kinds of measures taken in product manufacture. The approach here is to develop and regulate a good *quality control* (QC) program. The QC program involves monitoring all stages of the manufacturing process in which value is added to the product. Such monitoring requires that both the product and the equipment used in the various stages of production perform in accordance with established standards. This means that all instrumentation and calibration devices used to check tolerance or performance should be traceable to the specifications of the National Bureau of Standards or other accepted authority. Where *nondestructive inspection* (NDI) techniques are used, such as ultrasonics, radiography, or magnetic particle methods, these techniques should be applied under strict adherence to standards of good practice. Whenever the QC program discloses a problem, efforts should be made to determine the cause of the malperformance and to rectify it.

Beyond the measures outlined above to protect against product liability in the design and manufacture stages, the producer should carry adequate liability insurance. These policies should identify specifically who (individuals and/or organization) is insured thereunder, and under what circumstances. As with all insurance policies, liability insurance should be audited and updated regularly to ensure its sufficiency in the face of current protection needs.

In 1972 the federal government passed the Consumer Product Safety Act establishing the Consumer Product Safety Commission. The purpose of the Commission is to create and enforce safety standards relating to all consumer products except firearms, boats, motor vehicles, and aircraft. In addition to this particular responsibility, the Commission is also charged with enforcing other congressional acts, including the Flammable Fabrics Act, the Federal Hazardous Substances Act, the Poison Prevention Packaging Act, and the Refrigerator Safety Act.

Also of importance in the field of consumer protection is the Magnuson-Moss Warranty–Federal Trade Commission Improvement Act. This act provides minimum disclosure standards for written consumer product warranties, defines minimum federal content standards for such warranties, and amends the Federal Trade Commission Act in order to improve consumer protection activities.

The federal government is continuing to undertake legislation to regulate products, services, and systems used by the public. Such legislation is intended to serve the dual purpose of protecting the public from faulty design or production and protecting industry from the sometimes fatally large sums awarded in damage suits. This second aspect is particularly important in high-technology industry, where exposure to lawsuits involving huge claims can and does impede technological progress by stifling innovative design.

Future legislation will undoubtedly exempt producers of advanced technological systems, such as aerospace systems, from common law recovery actions based on negligence and will replace present law with laws that set definite limits on damage recovery. At the present time many government R&D contracts often contain specific clauses that indemnify a contractor for any liability related to the product developed under contract. This tends to stimulate participation from R&D organizations that would otherwise decline to bid on certain contracts because of exposure to product liability litigation.

PROFESSIONAL PRACTICE LIABILITY

In recent years a legal trend has developed which is destined to have important consequences on the future practice of engineering and the applied sciences in the United States. This movement addresses the responsibility to be borne by engineers and consultants for the quality of their professional services. Following recent trends in the medical and legal professions, engineers increasingly are being held legally accountable for their work: in the 15-year-period 1960–1975, the rate of claims against engineers has doubled. Those most vulnerable to liability suits are practitioners engaged in designing systems involving substantial capital investment and in which public safety is at stake. Structural engineers have the highest claim rate, but the problem also faces other engineering specialties, consulting firms, and research laboratories that provide advice and design data to clients. Basic R&D activities—in which applications are only potential and long-range—are essentially immune.

The legal basis for liability suits lies in the concept that a professional should be held accountable for his negligence and/or incompetence. Of the two faults, *incompetence*—the lack of adequate qualifications or abilities to perform to accepted standards—is the easier to address. Nevertheless, it is difficult to prove incompetence in court except in the most blatant cases, for the allegation is subjective and relative. Furthermore, approval of design work or advice by an engineer who is duly registered and licensed to practice by appropriate state or national authority virtually eliminates liability through incompetence in most cases of practical interest. To an increasing extent, professional registration is being recognized as a definition of competency.*

Negligence is a more difficult charge to defend against. It is often taken to mean anything short of the most exhaustive and exacting conformity to standards, whereas practical realities of time and cost nearly always demand that some sacrifice in testing and analysis be accepted in favor of sound technical judgment. No specific contingency or potential anomaly in materials, assembly, geological characteristics, environment, and other parameters can be accounted for with 100 percent assurance, since systems confidence is essentially a stochastic quality. Nevertheless, it is a fact that, in the majority of legal suits brought against engineers, some negligence has been proved to the satisfaction of the courts.

In some instances the engineer may be subject to prosecution under conditions where *strict liability* applies. Strict liability embraces the concept that a professional should be held liable if his work is deficient, without the need to prove his negligence or intent. The courts thus far have rejected strict liability in most cases involving engineering designers. However, recent trends in medical malpractice suits suggest that the door may one day be opened to strict liability litigation in connection with technical design work.

The engineer can exercise self-protection by practicing defensively in two general directions. The first of these has to do with contract language. More attention is being paid to current interpretations of traditional contract wording. Construction engineers who are contractually required to "design and supervise" their projects, and who, for reasons of cost, are limited in the amount of time they can spend in on-site supervision, have been held liable for construction deficiencies that are normally considered to be the fault of the contractor. Thus the trend has

---

* Indeed, the trend toward professional registration is also being seen in the field of management. Managers from professional groups in Great Britain, Greece, and West Germany have recently established codes of professional management conduct to define and regulate their practice.

been toward replacing the wording "design and supervise" with "provide advice" in order to reduce the engineer's responsibility for such errors.

Another area of contract language that is undergoing change concerns the guarantee of performance. Here again the engineer's responsibility for backing the guarantee can be cushioned by giving the client assurance that the construction "to the best of the design professional's knowledge, information, and belief" will meet specifications. In this way the client is called upon to share the burden of risk for the project with the contractor. Obviously, engineers remain responsible for cost-cutting actions that could be held unwise or dangerous if not justified by sound technical judgment. One of the best safeguards against legal allegations of negligence is through the strict adherence to accepted test procedures or design practices where applicable—although "accepted" procedures and practices are admittedly difficult to define.

The second way in which the engineer can practice defensively is to maintain records thoroughly and orderly. This caveat applies not only to chronologies of technical data and calculations but also to memoranda and correspondence which can help to reconstruct the evolution of a project if the need to do so should arise. Bound notebooks of technical results should be kept where possible, and should be signed and dated as information is entered. Instruments and test equipment should be calibrated by certified inspectors at regular intervals using instruments that are in turn traceable back to approved standards.

Liability insurance, of course, is yet another option open to the employer or private consultant. Unfortunately, carriers of professional liability insurance are few and the policies quite expensive and rapidly escalating. Many entrepreneurs with potential exposure to liability litigation find that they either cannot afford insurance or fail to meet eligibility criteria. Up-to-date information on the subject of professional liability insurance can be obtained through the National Society of Professional Engineers or the American Consulting Engineers Council, both of which are headquartered in Washington, D.C.

Managers of R&D enterprises whose business is potentially

susceptible to litigation have a responsibility to inform all staff members of such exposure, both personal and organizational. Serious consideration ought to be given to setting up procedures or guidelines to be followed by the technical staff to reduce future legal risk. Frank discussion between management and staff will elevate overall understanding of the problem, help dispel misconceptions, and aid in developing a defensive practice posture. Meanwhile, as the entire issue of professional liability continues to develop it is likely that responsibility will shift to the point where the buyer of the services (usually, the public at large) will assume a share of the risk, thus eventually lessening the burden on the profession.

REFERENCES

1. D. Allison (Ed.), *The R&D Game: Technical Men, Technical Managers, and Research Productivity*, Chapter 19. Cambridge, Mass.: M.I.T. Press, 1969.
2. W. H. Riemer, *Handbook of Government Contract Administration*. Englewood Cliffs, N.J.: Prentice-Hall, Inc., 1968.
3. *Government Contracts Reporter*, Commerce Clearing House, Inc., 4025 W. Peterson Ave., Chicago, Ill. 60646.
4. J. E. Goldman, "Basic Research in Industry," in *The R&D Game: Technical Men, Technical Managers, and Research Productivity*, edited by D. Allison. Cambridge, Mass.: M.I.T. Press, 1969, pp. 198–211.
5. T. W. Jackson and J. M. Spurlock, *Research and Development Management*, Chapter 9. Homewood, Ill.: Dow Jones–Irwin, Inc., 1966.
6. W. F. Glueck, and R. A. Mittelstaedt, "Protecting Trade Secrets in the '70's," *California Management Review*, Fall 1973, pp. 34–39.
7. R. M. Milgrim, "Get the Most Out of Your Trade Secrets," *Harvard Business Review*, November/December 1974, pp. 105–112.

ANNOTATED BIBLIOGRAPHY

Several of the more important recent books which address various aspects of technological management are described in brief below, and are listed chronologically from the most recent. While no such list can be complete, it should be useful to the reader wishing to consult other references in the field. Also, the reader should not overlook the references at the end of each chapter of this book; many contain valuable information on specialized topics.

> *Science and Technology: Vital National Resources,* edited by Ralph Sanders. Mt. Airy, Md.: Lomond Books, 1975. 146 pages.

A collection of six chapters dealing with the nature and dimensions of R&D and the role of the federal government in the R&D process. Chapter 3 ("Managing Research and Development Activities," by Ivan Asay) touches in condensed form many of the subjects treated in the present book.

> *Managing Technological Innovation,* by Brian C. Twiss. London: Longman Group, Ltd., 1974. 236 pages.

This book is written for senior managers of R&D firms, whether in the area of marketing, finance, production, or R&D. Its eight chapters focus on such issues as R&D policy and strategy, decision making, financial performance, planning and control, and organization for innovation. It is well written and thoroughly referenced.

> *Effective Management of Research and Development,* by Arthur Gerstenfeld. Reading, Mass.: Addison-Wesley Publishing Co., 1970. 150 pages.

In this monograph the author presents and analyzes the findings of his and others' research into the management policies of R&D managers and into R&D marketing strategies. It describes corporate R&D policy, R&D marketing, creativity and information flow, and decision making and information flow. It is best suited for higher-level management and others seeking a background in the broad aspects of the R&D management process.

Fundamentals of Research Management, by William G. McLoughlin. New York: American Management Associations, 1970. 245 pages.

In its 11 tightly written chapters, this book addresses project promotion, planning, and management, as well as such related areas as budgeting and technological forecasting. It is aimed at all levels of management, stressing research as an investment requiring proper management.

The R&D Game: Technical Men, Technical Managers, and Research Productivity, edited by David Allison. Cambridge, Mass.· The M.I.T. Press, 1969. 322 pages.

This book consists of three parts: The Man, The Environment, and The Organization. Its 19 chapters, written by an outstanding collection of scientists, social psychologists, and R&D corporate executives, cover several areas developed in Chapters 1, 3, and 4 of the present book. Some key topics are creativity, innovation, supervision, basic research and technology, and the federal government's role in research.

Managing Engineering and Research, 2d edition, by Delmar W. Karger and Robert G. Murdick. New York: Industrial Press, Inc., 1969. 534 pages.

This book, written for engineering managers, parallels the contents of the present book in several respects. Its four parts broadly address business strategy and the nature of management, organizational structure and staffing, program development and implementation, and finally several miscellaneous topics including certain legal and administrative aspects of R&D activities. It contains considerable detail, and has a distinctively "how to" orientation that many readers may find useful.

Management Guide for Engineers and Technical Administrators, edited by Nicholas P. Chironis. New York: McGraw-Hill Book Co., 1969. 376 pages.

This book contains a collection of articles, previously published in *Product Engineering* and similar journals, written by more than 80 senior engineering managers. It is perhaps the closest publication to a handbook for the beginning manager yet issued: specific, pragmatic, easy to read, and extensively illustrated. It is suited to the production-oriented engineer interested in learning about basic management techniques.

Research and Development Management: The Economics and Administration of Technology, by Daniel D. Romans. Englewood Cliffs, N.J.: Prentice-Hall, Inc., 1968. 450 pages.
The author has treated many areas of the R&D management process of importance to the mid-level manager. His book is the single most comprehensive treatment yet published and serves as a companion to the present one, especially the first four chapters.

Research and Development Management, by T. W. Jackson and J. M. Spurlock. Homewood, Ill.: Dow Jones-Irwin, Inc., 1966. 232 pages.
This book consists of nine chapters and focuses on the generation of R&D projects, conducting them through proper management of human resources, and reporting and utilizing the results. It is useful reading for both senior-level professionals and section managers who wish additional background in management of R&D projects.

Research, Development, and Technological Innovation: An Introduction, by James R. Bright. Homewood, Ill.: Richard D. Irwin, Inc., 1964. 783 pages.
This book consists of selected readings and case studies, organized into five sections: The Process of Technological Innovation; Case Studies in Research, Development, and Technological Innovation; Finding and Evaluating Significant Technological Opportunities; On the Use of Advanced Technology; and Technological Planning and Forecasting. The cases provide a good didactic experience for the classroom, while the readings cover a very broad spectrum of R&D management thought.

The Research and Development Engineer as Manager, by Thomas Moranian. New York: Holt, Rinehart and Winston, 1963. 152 pages.
This book addresses the R&D project leader's role with respect to the budgetary process. It is based on experience drawn from the electronics industry, but is pertinent to any multidisciplinary field of R&D in which the budget process must integrate the needs of pure and applied research, development engineering, and pilot production.

INDEX

deep-pockets theory of tort
liability, 208
Delphi method, 168
democratic style of management,
85
departmentalization principle,
27–29
deserter style of management, 82,
83
design defects in products,
207–209
developer style of management,
82, 83
directing, manager role in, 16
dissatisfiers (hygiene factors),
71–73
Divita, S. F., 147
Drucker, Peter, 18, 84n, 105, 109
dual advancement ladder,
100–102
dual authority system, 25

economic development, R&D for,
10, 11
economic system, planned
obsolescence and
international, 137
Edison, Thomas, 86
education programs to combat
obsolescence, 103–105
educational institutions, R&D by,
6
effectiveness, managerial, 80,
81–83
employment contracts, 205–206
engineers
in research and development,
illustrated, 12
see also high-talent personnel
evaluation process
for patentability, 196–197
of R&D proposals, 162–163,
164, 165–166
exception principle, 25

executive style of management,
82, 83
expenditures for R&D, 8, 9, 11
exploratory forecasting, 168

facial expressions, as modes of
nonverbal communication,
115, 116
Faraday, Michael, 86
Federal Contract Research
Centers (FCRC), R&D
through, 4
Federal Procurement Regulations
(FPR), 180–181, 183
(illustrated), 184
feedback, inadequate, and failure
of management by objectives,
110
firm-fixed-price contracts (FFP),
192
fixed-price contracts, 185, 191–
194
fixed-price-with-escalation
contracts, 192
fixed-price-incentive contracts,
193
fixed-price-level-of-effort
contracts, 194
forcing, in handling conflict, 49
forecasting
approaches to, 166–171
see also technological planning
and forecasting
foreign licensing (technical
assistance), 202n
formal advertising, procurement
by, 179–180
formal organization theory, 21–32
authority system in, 22–23; see
also authority
basic management principles in,
23–31
bureaucratic structure in, 31–32;
see also bureaucracy

3-D theory *(continued)*
  four basic managerial styles, 81
  3-D diagram, 83
three-skill model, 73–74, 75, 76
time-and-materials contracts
  (T&M), 185, 194–195
Toffler, Alvin, 1
top-down costing process, 161
trade secrets, 203–206
trademarks, 202, 203
training by objectives, 103
trend analysis, 168
Truman Harry S., 25
Twedt, D., 103*n*

unenforceable contracts, 187
unity-of-command principle,
  24–25

valid contracts, 187
Vettler, Eric W., 123
voidable contracts, 187

warranties, product, 207
Weber, Max, 31–32
Wilemon, D. L., 48
withdrawal, in handling conflict,
  49
work challenge factors, and
  motivation of high-talent
  personnel, table, 93
work pressures, 93–95
Wright, Orville, 140
Wright, Wilbur, 140
written communication, 116–119

X, theory, 65–69, 78, 85

Y, theory, 65–69, 78, 85